THE

RELUCTANT

ALCHEMIST

Lila Das
through
Cathryn Jones

ISBN: 978-1-913479-57-2 (paperback)
ISBN: 978-1-913479-58-9 (ebook)

That Guy's House
20-22 Wenlock Road
London
England
N1 7GU
www.thatGuysHouse.com

"The union of opposites is the focus of the alchemist… it is the tension between the opposites that allows one to grow or transform…the final union of dark and light is transformation or perfection." - **Carl Jung**

"My path to enlightenment started because I hated my thighs." - **Cathryn Jones**

My Gratitude Page(s)

For that is what it truly is… in black and white I want to express how deeply grateful I am to all the people in my life. Without each and every one of you, from my parents to the un-named lady I sat next to on the plane, I would not be here now. Even if this is your first encounter with me, I thank you from the bottom of my heart. I thank you. Thank you for being the light (or darkness) that you are and thank you for teaching me.

My parents have put up with me the longest, at least in this lifetime. I have given them a lot of reason to lose sleep over the years, and this book isn't likely to alleviate that situation. So, Mom and Dad, my apologies in advance, I love you and I am deeply grateful for all the amazing opportunities and support you have given me through the years. My brother, Lee, who is an amazing human being and soul who really understands what unconditional love is. I am lucky to have him as a touchstone and fellow traveler on this road (and grateful to him for bringing Tina into our lives… another awesome bright light!).

My ex-husband, Jim, also gets credit for putting up with me for a really long time. He is the father of my beloved children and that would be reason enough to thank him…

but he has also been the most amazing ex-husband ever and without his support this book would not have happened. Note here that Morgan's husband in the book is NOT Jim. Some of the circumstances may be the same, but the character is not at all him. I would also like to thank Jim's family for being the loving and wonderful creatures they are: Meredith Rowland, Stephen Rowland, Maggie, Harley and of course, Emee and BJ. And I can thank him for sweet Zina, a new addition to the family.

My kids, my beautiful, uniquely talented, passionate, loving, creative kids…James and Vivian, my heart bursts with gratitude and love when I think of the two of you. What amazing people you have grown into…I am grateful to the AllOne for allowing me to participate in your extraordinary lives. I have not always lived up to my own ideals as a parent, but please never doubt that I love you more than I could ever express. I will never be a talented enough writer to capture the depth of feeling I have for my two very special angels.

My earthly guides I thank for their patience, their wisdom and showing me how to not take things so seriously…Shomit Mitter, thank you for seeing me and showing myself to me, and thank you for introducing me to the "real" world. And thank you for helping me to understand that I wasn't losing my mind! In truth you played a pivotal role in this chapter of my life, but in attempting to tell the story, you and my spirit guide became one, which is probably just as it should be! And

I know you will appreciate that. David Furlong, who knew how much fun spirit release could be?! And the magical trip through Egypt was not only a spiritual experience but a hell of a ride (and a lot of fun), and my first conscious experience with manifestation.

Vera Lester, my spiritual counselor and coach for the last several years who has held my hand, encouraged me, channeled with me…I could not have survived the last few years without your insights and support.

My favorite Irish writing teacher, Stephen Rea, thank you for the good times, the good counsel, and a party every Thursday in writing class. I cannot see an "ly" word without thinking of you. My writing group who did their best to keep me and this story somewhat grounded: Frank and Rose Peterson, Archie Hovenesian, Dana Moyer and of course, Macon Fry. Thank you Macon, for all the love, support and patience as well as writing guidance - this book would not be readable without your help: "I dunno…I think you might need to cut down on the number of weird creatures in here…"

A host of friends who kept me going through some tough times over the last six years, whether it was a glass of wine, a chat on the phone, a long walk, a good yoga class or taking the time to read my book: Dee McCloskey, Ashbrooke Tullis, John Ormond, Aimee Freeman, Carl Phyfer, Lisa Smit, Eileen McMahon, Mitchel Bleier, Brandy Asch, Rae Bryan, Ashley Nolan, Michele Johnston, Meredith Rowland, Hans

Jonassen, Veronica Rubio, Pippa Neve, Bill Loehfelm, AC Lambeth, Andra Aiken, Sean Johnson and the Wild Lotus team. Tanya Arler who saw me from day one and never gave up on me! Tanya also introduced me to my very patient publisher, Sean Patrick at That Guy's House Publishing… I hope he doesn't have a heart attack when I finally turn this in. I also want to thank Celerina Manongdo who stuck with us through thick and thin, loved my children like her own, and put up with me for over 10 years.

The best neighbors ever, Garland Robinette and Nancy Rhett. Not only are they great people, but Garland was one of my precious readers and, more importantly, generously offered to allow me to use one of his fabulous paintings as my cover art. How lucky am I?

And anyone I forgot, I'll catch you on the flip side… Ooops, I almost forgot the most important thank you of all! The AllOne and the cast of characters who are my guides… thank you for all the love, the lessons and most of all for allowing me to be an instrument, a conduit for your work… may my gratitude and devotion increase with each passing day. Thank you.

Much Love,
Cathryn

Prologue

Three things Morgan heard when she was a child: you will write a book about religion; you will be a priest; you will save the world. It was not her parents who told her these things. It was her imaginary friends, the ones in her head who spoke to her all the time. They comforted her when she was sad. They played games with her like "hide and seek" and "make the wind blow". They told her stories about other times that she had lived.

One story they often told her was about the girl who left her father's house and followed a strange man with magical powers. The story was set long ago when there were no cars and people wore funny clothes. Her imaginary friends (that's what her mother called them) didn't just tell her stories; they showed her stories. Often, just as she was going to sleep or waking up, they would play what they called, "one of their movies." She felt like she wasn't just watching these stories, she was part of them, as if they were real.

In one of her favorites, she got to dress up like a knight and go charging about. Yet it always began the same way, as a young girl dreaming on a hill:

She looked out across the rolling hills past her sheep. The sun was on it's final blaze before setting. Gazing toward the horizon she spied a dust tail rising on the road. Men on horses, moving fast. God told her this man would come.

He came to ask if the rumors and accounts were true. Did she really know things about people she had never met before? Did she predict the future? She sat leaning against the tree watching the dust tail resolve into horses with people on them. She saw their weapons glint in the setting sun. The armed men turned off the road and headed into the field to progress toward the hill on which she sat waiting.

She did not move. Her sheep, threatened by the noise and bluster of the large horses, protested the arrival of the men with startled bleats. Their bells clanked as they scattered in several directions, opening a path toward her. She took a deep breath and waited.

Five armoured men came to a halt at the foot of the hill. The lead horse, an enormous white one that must have been

12 hands high, tossed its head as his rider dismounted. Her scratchy shift and apron offered little protection against the armour and weapons of these men. But she was not scared. She knew God was on her side; she trusted the voices within. Voices within told her there was no threat here, all would be as it should. She stood dusting her hands off on her dress as the leader approached. She made no move toward him.

He removed his helmet as he trudged up the hill, armour crunching all the way. Long dark hair rested on his shoulders and piercing blue eyes caught hers as he came closer.

"Are you Joan?" he asked.

"I am."

"You are the maid who tells the future?"

"I don't tell the future, God does."

"God speaks to you?"

"Yes."

"And why would God speak to you little maid?"

"Because I listen."

It got more exciting after that, but she loved the way it began and, in all honesty, she thought the man with the long dark hair and blue eyes was very handsome. There was something about him that made her breathless. He often appeared in various "movies" that her imaginary friends played for her. He would look different and wear other costumes, but she always knew him when she looked into his eyes. Her imaginary friends told her she would meet him again someday because... well, just because.

Morgan stopped listening to those voices in her head when she realized there were boys she wanted to kiss, when she got caught up in school, and then got married and started having children, realized her dream of helping others as a social worker and then abandoned this calling to follow her husband's job to a handful of foreign lands.

She was no longer a child. She knew she was never going to write a book, much less one about religion; what did she know? There were no women priests in her church - that was not allowed. Saving the world? Obviously they had to be wrong about that too, so they must just be the childish imaginary friends her mother told her they were. She stopped listening to them and they went away. Or so she thought.

London, UK

2011

Day 1

Morgan stared into her closet and wished every single piece of clothing would burst into flames. Except for the jeans folded neatly on the floor. The jeans were the only piece of clothing that really fit her. All the fancy dresses, the designer shoes, the bags, they were all part of an elegant masquerade. And she was supposed to put on a costume and go out with "the wives". She flicked through the dresses waiting on the cloth hangers like girls hoping for a chance to dance. Her hand settled on baby soft cloth. With relief she pulled the shapeless black dress out of the closet and tossed it onto the bed.

"Is that what you're wearing to Nobu tonight?" Rachel leaned against the stiff pillows on Morgan's overwrought bed and raised an eyebrow.

"I'm going tonight because I miss Deborah... and because you're coming. Ben won't be there to judge me."

Morgan stepped back into the bright, white, marble bathroom. She leaned forward into the mirror as she

1

raised her dark brows and applied mascara with quick, thoughtless, strokes. Her grey-blue eyes regarded her in the mirror. She tried to focus and not think too much. Her life had become a fog of "have-to's". She pulled her wavy blonde-highlighted hair in a sort of bun and clipped it with a comb as Rachel went on.

"That's true…where is he anyway?"

On cue, Morgan's phone danced on the coverlet. She picked it up. "Hey… No… That's fine… Remember I have dinner with the bank girls tonight… I know… Tomorrow? Ok…No, I 'll take care of it…Yeah… Thanks…Bye." She put the phone down on the bed.

"Apparently he's with Marie. The charade continues," said Morgan.

"He's not going to give you grounds for divorce on a silver platter…"

"He already has."

"So why are you still here?"

Nobu was a restaurant that owed its success to the culture of celebrity. If most of the patrons were not star-struck by the galaxy of famous owners, the place would have ceased to exist long ago. A snooty host spent 5 minutes shifting papers around her podium and ignoring her patrons before she acknowledged Morgan and Rachel.

She then guided them through the narrowest of passages throbbing with the sounds created by the clink and clatter of glassware, utensils and plates, cushioned by the voices and laughter of diners. Rachel grasped her hand and pulled Morgan through the crowd as if afraid she might run away. They stopped at the table of familiar faces, Morgan felt like a fraud.

"Morgan, I'm so glad you came… I hear it's hard to get you out these days," standing, Deborah reached out to hug Morgan. Tears sprang to Morgan's eyes as Deborah squeezed her.

"I didn't want to miss you while you were in town," said Morgan, grateful for the low lighting of the restaurant.

While Rachel moved in to greet Deborah, Morgan made the ritual round of the table greeting each of the other women. She felt as if there was a key she was missing to a lock she couldn't find. They sat down and ordered drinks from a black clad waitress who seemed ready to bolt before they finished their requests.

Morgan appreciated that these women understood the relentless nature of the seemingly glamorous lives they all led. Like Morgan, several of them had lived in Asian countries and understood the dirge of endlessly reinventing yourself in places where you loathed going to the grocery store because you could not face trying to communicate in a language so far from the French or Spanish offered in your high school that it did not even share the same alphabet. They shoe-horned unhappy kids into new schools every two years. They tried to keep marriages together in places where the custom was for corporate men to be "entertained" by scantily clad women who catered to their every whim.

The ladies at this table in particular knew that the "easy" move to a place where your language is spoken could be more isolating and difficult because now you don't even have the excuse of looking like you don't belong. So they sat in comfortable commonality taking advantage of the fact that they could enjoy a nice meal and celebrate their friendship and commiserate with difficulties no one else understood. This made Morgan more miserable because she did not feel worthy and wondered why these ladies tolerated her. They could put on the show. They could take advantage of the perks offered by the privileged setting and make it look easy.

"Oh shit," said Deborah, as the full champagne glass in her hand flipped pink liquid out into the middle of the table.

A man stood behind her and brushed her shoulders with a white napkin. "I'm… so… sorry… it's HIS fault," he said as he gestured to one of his companions across the table. "Let us buy you a round of drinks… what's that you had? Champagne?"

Deborah protested but the group of loud businessmen sent a bottle anyway.

Not five minutes later Deborah was knocked forward again. "Gosh these tables are so close together, sorry, I was just trying to get up." The sharp-featured man attempted a smile and then apologized again with two bottles of champagne.

More black clad servers interrupted spilled drinks and apologies bringing plates of blackened miso cod, bright pink tuna sashimi with eye-watering wasabi sauce, neon-green seaweed salad and warm salty miso soup.

Morgan struggled to keep up the game and stay in tune with the conversation at the table. In a fog, Morgan watched Deborah, Rachel and herself land at the table of the bumbling businessmen. The other three women ducked out early.

The man next to Morgan grabbed her hand and put it on his crotch. Jolted awake, Morgan thought, *"Shit. Is that a hard on? I was just talking about sweating in a hot yoga class...oh my god."* She snatched her hand away deciding it was time to go, and looked across the table to catch Rachel's eye and give her a distress signal. She almost screamed, "Let's get out of here now!" But Rachel's brown head was bent forward in deep conversation with a swarthy man whose chest hair crested out of his open shirt creating a black bushy forest around his gold chain. She did not see Morgan.

Morgan beheld the man seated opposite her. A paralyzing pair of navy blue eyes bewitched and transfixed her. All the glitzy noise of the restaurant collapsed into that one moment; the clink of glassware and china ceased, the hum of hundreds of voices died, the laughter next to and behind her disappeared. For the first time she knew what "time stopped" meant because it did and all that existed was Morgan and a pair of navy blue eyes burning through her soul.

Then a clear voice came into her head, "*Get up, say nothing, and wait for me downstairs.*"

"*Oh my God, is that guy talking to me again?*" thought Morgan. She broke the gaze lock and looked at crotch-man to see if he had whispered this proposition in her ear, but his back was to her as he now engaged himself in conversation with Deborah's ample breasts.

She looked up and across the table. Blue eyes still stared at her, an eyebrow arched in question.

The voice came back into her head, "*Did you not hear me? Get up. Say nothing. Meet me downstairs.*" Other than the smirk that worked its way across his face, his lips did not move.

Morgan stared back at him feeling like shattered glass. "*Am I crazy? Am I drunk? Or did this guy really just*

talk to me in my head? What is that called… telepathy?"
These thoughts whirled as she stared back at the man.

He cocked his head, smiled and then nodded. Feathers of steel grey hair framed the mischievous blue eyes. He leaned forward as he held her gaze, the voice more insistent now, **"*Get up. Say nothing. Meet me downstairs."*** And then, a moment later, **"*Please."***

Morgan rose from the table, shouldered her bag, said nothing to Mr. I-wish-you-would-feel-my-hard-on or her friends and went downstairs to the front door. Just as she thought, *"Ok, I imagined that"* the man with the blue eyes was beside her.

He took her by the arm and led her outside.

"I think we need to go somewhere else. Let's grab a taxi." A taxi pulled up to the door with a wave from the doorman. Her companion opened the door and held it for her. She ducked in and sat down. He followed.

To the driver he said, "Do you know where the All Bar One is near Leicester Square?" The driver answered with a nod.

Looking Morgan over with a wolfish smile he said, "God I can't believe we just fucking did that. We just left. Have you ever done anything like that?"

"No, never…" came out from somewhere south of her nose as she swam underwater and time again slowed down. *"This is not something I ever imagined myself doing,"* thought Morgan.

"We just left. Wow. I'm really glad to be away from those assholes. Jesus." He laughed and looked straight at her, "I don't even know your name."

"My name is Morgan. Morgan Gardiner."

"Jeff, nice to meet you," this came out with a sideways grin that was nearly a leer.

"Jeff…. what?"

"Oh, let's not worry about that right now. You know I watched you the whole time. You're amazing and gorgeous. You have the most wonderful eyes, I noticed you the moment you walked in the room."

Morgan answered with the silence in her head. Then she realized he was still speaking.

Looking at her left hand he said, "Based on the rings I presume you are married."

"Uhhhh…it's complicated."

"Complicated how?"

Her chest rose with a deep inhale. "Let's just say that my husband has a roving eye and has for a long time."

"And you…?"

"I go to church and make him look good."

That elicited a laugh. "I'm sure that's true…What does he do for a living? I bet whatever it is, he wears suits. I hate suits, don't even own one."

"He's a lawyer. You aren't married?"

"Divorced."

"Hmmmm…" London unfurled outside the window, black taxis with their round eyes, reverent architecture laced with lights and neon.

"Marriage isn't what it's cracked up to be, is it?" asked Jeff.

A laugh was surprised out of her; she smiled at her black furry flats and shook her head, "No, it's not what I thought it would be."

"So do you regularly end up in the beds of men you've just met?"

"I'm a 45 year old former social worker with two kids and a basset hound puppy, what do you think? And right now, we're in a taxi."

It was his turn to laugh. "No, you really don't seem like the type. What would the ladies back at Nobu think?"

"I just hope they didn't notice. I wouldn't want to explain it."

"We left separately… I don't think you've anything to worry about."

"How did we come to leave at the same time?" She questioned schizophrenic style hallucinations of cosmic connections in dark pseudo-Japanese restaurants.

He looked straight at her. His fierce blue eyes captured hers for a brief second, "Because I asked you to."

"But you didn't…"

They stopped. The door opened as she inhaled the question she was afraid to ask. Once out of the taxi, whinnying flatterers bobbed and weaved all around him drawn like iron shavings to a magnet. The bouncers at the door, the mini-cab drivers on the street all chorused with, "Oh Mr. Jeff, it's been so long, where have you been?" The ritual male dance of clutched forearms, slapped shoulders and shaken hands took place. She swam in a fish bowl and observed the exchange. *"Who the hell is he?"* she thought.

They stepped across the threshold into a bar that throbbed with people at least ten years younger than them. A crowd bounced in the center of a makeshift dance floor. A DJ occupied the space at the end of the bar behind a mound of equipment and blinking lights, his headphones askew so that one ear remained exposed.

Jeff slid an arm around her waist. "What do you want?"

"Water, please."

"You sure?"

"I don't need anything else to drink." She wanted her head to clear a bit.

"Okay." He turned and leaned over the dark bar toward the beefy bartender. She watched the kids on the dance floor and thought about the last time she had been one of them.

When she turned back to the bar there were ten bottles of water sweating in front of her. Jeff looked at her over his glass as he sipped a dark liquid poured over ice.

She opened one of the waters.

"I know it sounds like a line, but I really did notice you the moment you came into the room tonight. It's not just that you're pretty, there is so much more there and I could see it in you. I always can. You shine…"

She had no idea how to respond. She felt like the star of a bad soap opera.

A powerful forearm slid around her back and pulled her close. Blood rushed to her head and drowned out the music of the disco. Pressed up against him she could smell his cologne. She felt giddy. She could feel herself yield to him as his hands traced the curves of her chest, waist and hips, as he squeezed the sides of her body together like a child with a new plush toy. Then he smiled into her eyes and kissed her on the forehead. It was a sweet gesture, father-like.

"Who are you? Where did you come from? You have the most amazing energy… who are you?"

"I... I don't really know… I'm just Morgan. I think the better question is, who are you?"

He grinned down at her then, grabbing her hand, moved toward the crowd that undulated on the dance floor. "Let's dance."

It was hard to move much so they bounced with the crowd until they began to sweat.

"Can we go somewhere else?" Asked Morgan.

"Are you hungry?"

"No, not really."

"Can we go next door and get a kebab?"

"I guess."

"What exactly do you do?" He asked this question in between mouthfuls of gyro. She watched him as she teetered on an unbalanced stool.

"I'm a trailing spouse."

"A what? What the hell is that?"

"How to feel useless in two words or less. I follow my husband around from country to country. I move house, take care of the kids, get them settled in school and try to make everyone happy until it's time to move and we start the whole process again."

"How often does that happen?"

"Four countries and six houses in ten years. Bangkok, Seoul, Tokyo and now London."

"That's a lot of moving."

"The thought of a box makes me nauseous. My son told me he never wants to be the new kid again."

"My company wanted me to do that. I told 'em no way. So now I spend half my time living in a hotel room."

"Is that better?"

12

"I'm not sure. I still ended up divorced. How old are your kids?"

"Seven and twelve. You?"

"Boy and girl. Thirteen and fifteen." He wiped his mouth with a paper napkin and stuck a £20 note in the tip jar. "Are we going back to my hotel?"

"I guess."

A driver outside the bar had been waiting for Jeff. They got into the car. Jeff rolled up his sleeves to reveal tattooed forearms. "You see this? These are my kid's birth dates. And this," he said as he pointed to an image of a snake eating its tail, "well that's a story for another time."

They pulled into the circle in front of a hotel and he moved to get out as the door was opened for him. "Are you coming?"

"I don't know."

"Why don't you come up just for a little while?"

"I… I really think I need to get home."

He looked at her. "Ok, suit yourself." He slammed the door behind him and went for the hotel. She watched him hesitate and turn back as the taxi pulled away. Jeff whistled to get the guy to stop and walked up to the driver's window. The driver rolled the window down to receive a wad of bills. "Take her wherever she needs to go." With that he rapped loudly on the top of the cab and waved her off.

She realized she still did not know his last name.

"Christman... It's Christman." The voice in her head again. She turned around to see Jeff as he stood in the circle of the hotel driveway while she turned the corner on to Hyde Park. *"My last name is Christman."*

She sat back in the taxi and took a deep breath. Her entire body tingled in the same way it does when you think you might be about to see a ghost. Her heart pounded. She took another breath.

She arrived home in a cyclone of thoughts as she let herself in and closed the front door on the pink slurry skies of dawn. It was a school day. She would not get more than an hour of sleep at this point. She slipped off her shoes and padded on the balls of her feet so as not to wake the new puppy. The puppy whined in the kitchen below her. She had not been successful. She changed direction with a sigh and headed down the stairs.

The puppy thumped her tail against the wire crate and began to push at the door with her paw. Morgan lifted the latch and quickly opened the door to the patio. The pup rushed outside but turned when she heard the door shut behind her. Morgan watched through the glass as the dog loitered in the brick patio sniffing all the prime pee spots before she settled on the perfect place to squat.

Morgan opened the door. "Good girl, you're such a good little girl. Now let's get back in your crate for a bit longer, ok?"

The dog waited by the door of the crate until Morgan pulled a treat out of the box on the counter. She followed the treat into the crate and Morgan latched it shut. Her thoughts turned to her children asleep several floors above.

She drew herself up three flights of steps in the narrow townhouse and opened the door to Max's room to find him curled up with his now bald stuffed dog. Max's nose was firmly planted in its neck as he clutched the lovey to his chest.

She closed his door and crossed the hall to Daisy's room. Typical of Daisy, she had kicked off all the covers and was splayed in such a way that she took up every inch of the lower bunk bed. Morgan picked up the comforter and tucked it back around the sleeping child's body as best she could. She noticed the extra comforter and pillow on the ground near the closet and resisted the temptation to gather it up and put it back on the top bunk. Daisy insisted her imaginary friend, a boy in pink knickers, needed it to be on the floor.

Horse-like snoring sounds came from the nanny's room. Satisfied all was well, she took the stairs back down to the master bedroom.

Morgan opened the door to her room and sighed. Her white bed was still white and filled with overstuffed pillows. The sand colored carpet looked as fresh as it had hours ago when she and Rachel had left. The tan silk curtains hung languidly on the rods, artfully draping themselves across the floor.

She closed the door and pulled the soft black dress over her head as she crossed the room. She opened the doors to the closet to reach for a hanger and found there were no dresses in front of her, only hangers. She looked down and saw nothing but charred clumps on the floor. Heaps of ashes were all that remained of the designer dresses, shoes and bags. Every single piece of clothing was incinerated. She stuck her hand out over the ash heaps to test for heat, nothing. There was no acrid smell of smoke. The hangers hung empty on the rod. Then she saw the jeans. Her favorite pair of jeans lay folded on the floor just where they were before she left. They had not been touched.

Day 2

Morgan stood for a moment, struck by the carnage in the closet before her legs collapsed beneath her. *"What the fuck?"* As she sat on the floor she reached her hand out to test again for heat. The ashes were not even warm. She plunged her fingers under the black pile and lifted off some of the stuff to reveal a perfect carpet beneath. No fire. No smoke. No danger that this was about to turn into a conflagration, but no sign of how it happened.

She rinsed her hands before she went to her chest of drawers. Nothing in the chest was damaged. She went back to the closet, retrieved the jeans and slipped them on, then topped them with a long comfy sweater that did what it could to hide her curves.

Morgan slumped down on the edge of her bed. It was not long before she would have to get the kids up and get breakfast together before school. As she flipped through the images of the night like a picture book, exhaustion and disbelief hung around her shoulders like a moth-eaten mink stole.

The back and forth walk to school with the kids should have invigorated her, but she only felt tired.

She thought of Jeff again just as her phone sang Abba's *Dancing Queen* from the depths of her purse. "*I need to change that ringtone,*" she thought. She saw an unidentified number on the screen. She pressed the green button wondering if it was Jeff.

"Hello?"

"Mrs. Gardiner?" said an unfamiliar voice.

"Yes, this is she."

"Good morning. This is Yousef, the concierge at the Intercontinental Hotel Hyde Park. I have a package for you from a Mr. Christman. You can come get it here or we can send it over if you would kindly give me your address."

"Uhhh… I can come get it thanks. It will be at the desk?"

"Yes, Mrs. Gardiner. Thank you."

A frisson ran up her spine with the confirmation his last name was Christman. She started to feel nauseous. Morgan had no idea how long Jeff was supposed to be in London.

Possible telepathic communication with a stranger, her wardrobe in inexplicable ashes, almost cheating on her husband and getting the kids to school had distracted Morgan from eating. She went downstairs, toasted an English muffin, downed that with a diet coke and felt less nauseous.

The package hung in her mind like a chocolate bar squirreled away in the cabinet. The temptation was not lessened by a grocery list. She gave in, picked up her purse and headed out to Kensington High Street to find a cab. It was a straight shot up "Ken High Street" as the locals called it. Rows and rows of shops gave way to Kensington Gardens, Royal Albert Hall and then Hyde Park. Between the Regency buildings that faced the park you could catch glimpses of Knightsbridge and Harrods. The wide-eyed black cab turned the corner at "Number One, London". Morgan felt sick again. They pulled into the circle in front of the hotel, and she paid the driver. A bellhop held the door for her and she went in, to the concierge desk.

"May I help you?" asked the female at the desk.

"Ummm… my name is Morgan Gardiner. I got a call from you guys that I have a package?" Morgan fought the impulse to look around and see if Jeff was in the stream of people headed in and out of the hotel behind her.

"Yes, Mrs. Gardiner. I have it for you right here." She reached under the desk and handed Morgan a rectangular package about the size of a pack of cigarettes. It was wrapped in brown paper and had her name and telephone number on it.

"Thank you."

Caught in the revolving door at the entrance Morgan looked into the crowd for any sign of Jeff. She stepped out. The bellman looked at her and asked, "Taxi?"

"Yes please."

A black London cab responded to his whistle. "Where ya gone?"

"Scarsdale Villas. Kensington." She said as she ducked into the open door and sat on the wide seat.

She ripped open the paper from the package to reveal a cigarette box, Marlborough Lights. The pack was empty of cigarettes. Inside was a piece of crumpled cream-colored stationary. As she opened it her favorite pair of earrings fell into her lap. She reached up to touch her ears. The gold hoops she always wore were not there. *"When did I lose those?"* she thought. A note was written on the hotel stationary.

Found these in my pocket this morning. Thought you might want them back. If you want to contact me, the number is 426-555-2323. And the name is Christman. You can look it up. I have to be out of London for a few days, but I would like to see you when I get back. I leave it to you to get in touch with me if you are up for that. Jeff

She sank into the seat of the taxi and watched the shoppers walk along the High Street, bags in hand. She put the earrings on and stuffed the note into her purse as she considered her list for the day. Routine things like, what to make for dinner, school pick-ups, bills, kid activities. These were the things she was used to, not "how did this strange man who may have communicated with me in my head end up with earrings I did not know I lost?"

"Ahem... uhhh... lady... Scarsdale Villas? Which number?"

"Oh, sorry. Right. Seventy-nine, the block before Earl's Court Road."

Morgan paid the driver and got out of the car. She went upstairs and attempted a nap. But her whirling mind contained too many unanswered questions to allow for that. She looked Jeff Christman up on the internet.

Her computer exploded with information. He was the rhythm guitarist for the 80's band I AM. How many times had she danced to their music in high school and college or sung harmony with a carload of friends? The focus had been on Aaron, the lead singer. No one ever remembers the rhythm guitarist in a band. She saw that Jeff had started a successful record company after the band broke up. She followed him on Twitter. His latest tweet gushed about lunch at a pub outside of London.

Morgan tore herself away from the public version of Jeff's life on Wikipedia (no picture of the ex) to retrieve the children from school. The sour hours of homework and then the relief of dinner followed. After Morgan got the children bathed and tucked in, she found her husband in the closet full of ashes.

"What the fuck?" he asked.

"I've no idea. I left, the closet was fine. I came home, it's in ashes. No heat. No nothing, just ashes." She decided not to mention the jeans.

"Well, that doesn't help anything. What do we say to the landlord?"

"I don't know, I'll get an electrician out here tomorrow." Said Morgan.

"We need to talk," he said as he slammed the closet door shut. "I thought I should come home before you were asleep."

"Ok." Morgan followed him downstairs to the basement den next to the kitchen. He poured himself a glass of red wine and flopped onto the sofa. Morgan sat in her favorite chair with her feet propped up on the ottoman. "So, do you still have a job?"

He cocked his head and looked at her through narrowed eyes, "Yeah. But we've lost the ex-pat package. They just gave me the details today. We need to look for a new place to live now. They stop paying rent when the lease is up in August. Ideally we get out of here before that because then we can keep the difference to help with moving expenses."

"They aren't even going to pay for movers?"

"I'm still negotiating with them about that."

"So what's my budget?" asked Morgan.

"I'm still crunching the numbers. But I'll give it to you soon. For now, let's say it's less than half of what you have now for the next year, then nothing after that, from the company anyway."

"What about the kids' schools?"

"We get half the money for the next year. So Max can go on to Marlborough as planned. I'm figuring the rest out."

"I need to know in the next few days what kind of money we are talking about so I can call Olivia and look for a new place."

"I know. I'm going outside for a minute and then I've got some work to do."

Morgan said nothing; she guessed he wanted to sneak a cigarette on the patio now that the kids were in bed.

Morgan went back upstairs and got in bed with her computer. Ben would not be back up for a while. She pulled out the note with Jeff's number.

Morgan texted him: Hey. Thanks for the earrings.

She picked up her computer in an attempt to not obsessively check for a response.

When Morgan awoke, the computer was on the floor, the phone on the bedside table. Ben snored next to her in the bed.

Morgan picked up the phone. A text waited.

Jeff: Hey back. Glad you got in touch. I will call you tomorrow.

Day 3

"I'm sorry to tell you that there is nothing wrong with your electrics. I've no idea why all that stuff burned up. Mebbe one of your kids put a match to it?"

Morgan signed the bill for £150 and closed the front door behind the electrician. Questions flitted through her mind like gnats buzzing too close to her face. The answer that kept occurring made no sense.

As promised Jeff called later that morning. She walked out of the neighborhood Indian grocery store and stood on the sidewalk to talk to him.

"I'm really glad you got in touch. I was afraid you wouldn't."

"I'm still not sure it's a good idea... but, I have a lot of questions." She said.

"Let's have dinner then. And maybe we can talk about some of those questions. I get back to town on Tuesday. How about Tuesday night?"

"I'm married."

Jeff laughed. "I do remember that. It's ok. No hanky panky. Just dinner. I really need... I really want to talk to you... have a conversation. I also remember that you have the most amazing eyes. I want you across a table from me again. Please."

"Mr. Christman. Ahhhhhh." She lost that battle with herself. "OK, I guess."

"Great. I'll call you Monday. Bye."

Day 4

Morgan stalked Jeff on Twitter while he was outside of London. Most of the posts were about his business or what he just ate. She checked her phone like a rat feverishly pressing a lever in hope of a random treat. She wondered if he was on a date. She played games with herself. She lost each time.

A vision of a car accident accosted her as she sat on the tube and tried not to check her twitter feed. The scene played like a movie in her head. She saw a silver Mercedes SUV as it crossed an intersection. She saw a white Toyota t-bone the Mercedes. It was as if she floated above the intersection and had a view from all angles. She saw figures in the car, but she did not know them nor did she recognize the intersection. She was sure Jeff's daughter was in the back of the wrecked Mercedes. She texted him.

Morgan: I know this sounds crazy, but has your daughter been in an accident?

He did not return the text for several hours. Instead, he called.

"How the fuck did you know that my daughter was in an accident?"

"Are you serious?" Morgan sat down at the dining room table.

"Yes, I'm fucking serious. How did you know?"

"Jeff, I honestly have no idea. I was on the tube and all of sudden I had this vision of an intersection. I watched a Mercedes truck get hit by a white Toyota. Then somehow I knew it was your daughter. I don't even know her name. But I saw her in a car, and I saw that car get hit by another car. Is she ok?"

Morgan heard Jeff inhale at the other end of the line, "She will be, it's lucky she had her seatbelt on. Her twin was with them, but he was on the other side of the car and wasn't hurt. My ex was driving. They were t-boned by some shit who'd been drinking all night. My daughter has a broken arm, a bruised face and is pretty shaken up, but she's ok."

"And your ex?"

"I think there was more damage from the airbag than the accident with her. She's got a couple of cracked ribs and some bad bruises, but she's ok too."

"I'm glad they're ok."

"Me too."

"Jeff, I've no idea how I came up with this. How I knew. This scares me."

"I think I have an idea, but I don't have time to go into it now. I gotta go. If you get anything else like that call me, ok. Bye." He hung up.

She stared at the phone in her hand unable to believe what had just happened. She was not sure what upset her more - the inexplicable vision or the fact that Jeff had just blown her off again with no explanation. She felt like a child who had lost its mother in a crowd. And what the hell did he mean by, "if you get anything else like this"?

Day 5

The cave was not deep. She sat on a rectangular piece of stone shackled to the wall with large chains. The watermarks on the walls indicated that the water would be much higher with the tide, but it did not appear she would drown. It must be something else. She leaned against the wall and shivered in the chill of the cave as she watched the sparkling dance of sunlight on the water only yards away.

The sound of a roar somewhere nearby roused her from her reverie. It sounded almost like an animal. Almost. And again; the sound of a tortured soul or a person in great pain. She pulled her legs up and tried to shrink against the back of the cave. She could hear something slosh through the water.

A shadow appeared at the mouth of the cave. It had the head of a wolf and the body of a man. A high-pitched scream emanated from the creature and echoed into the cave. She pressed herself against the wall. It moved toward her. As it came closer she could see that a man wore the skin of a wolf, the head half covered his face. He was naked. She had never seen a naked man before. But she had been told. He was aroused. Sweat shone in the dim light. Fists clenched and unclenched in an unknown rhythm. He waded through the water, his breath forced and loud as though he ran.

He came closer. She could smell him. He reached out to grab her. She flinched and moved as far away as she could with the shackles holding her in place. He took one wrist and with the other hand released her from the shackles but not his grip. He climbed up on the rock and over her.

He ripped the white shift from her body with his teeth and then licked her. He licked her everywhere… her breasts, her stomach, between her legs. He never released her wrists. Then he rose over her once more and with a loud scream plunged into her. She barely had time to register this fact before he began to bite her, to tear off pieces of her flesh.

Morgan woke breathless with her t-shirt glued to her body with sweat, the images plastered in her mind like frescoes. *The wolf man in the dream was Jeff. And he consumed me,"* she thought.

Day 6

Wedged into a child-sized chair, nursing a headache, Morgan watched as Maria, the lead First Communion teacher, wrestled with the questions of intelligent children who spent more time watching horror movies than going to church.

"So Miss Maria, are we like vampires or something? If we're drinking blood, doesn't that make us vampires?"

Maria looked at the child with her wide, chocolate-coloured Filipina eyes... she did not blink. This was one of those questions not covered in the Holy First Communion instructor training classes. A rictus-like smile cemented itself in place until she composed herself. Morgan was grateful to be in the back of the classroom in her status as junior teacher, which meant chief-hander-outer-of-pencils.

"Well... Cecilia... no... uhhhhhh... it doesn't make us vampires..."

This child shark smelled transubstantiated wine in the water and she went for it, "but we are drinking blood..."

"No... yes, but it's... Christ's blood... that... he... uhhhhh... wants us to have."

"So does the priest use magic to turn it into blood?"

32

"Uhhhh... no magic is something else... the priest uses prayers..."

"How is that different?"

"It just is. You just have to believe me about this." Maria was determined to take the control back from the precocious child who threatened the very fabric of the Roman Catholic faith in her almost innocent seven-year-old way. "We are not vampires. The wine becomes the blood of Christ..."

"Does it taste like blood? I licked a cut on my arm once and I didn't like it. I don't want any blood." This came from a blonde boy at another table. Now the giggling started. The hunters sensed fear in the prey.

"You don't have to take the cup if you don't want to. A lot of people don't for a lot of different reasons. You just have to understand what we, as Catholics, believe. We believe in 'transubstantiation', which means that in the Mass, the prayers of the priests turn the bread and wine into the body and blood of Christ. He sacrificed himself for us, but He is still with us. That's what you need to know. Just remember what it means please. Who can repeat to me the meaning of 'transubstantiation?'" Hands shot up into the air as she smiled at the group. She pointed to a normally quiet little girl with curly hair.

"Transubstan... shiaaashun... is, is when the bread and wine become the body and blood of Jesus." She smiled. She was just glad to have gotten the word out.

"Very good. So when Father Paul comes in to see how we are doing, any of you could tell him that, right?"

"Yes, Miss Maria…" the group chorused back. She had whipped the hounds back into shape and averted certain disaster.

After class, Morgan and Daisy went to find Max in the courtyard garden of the church where they served coffee and cookies between the masses.

"Mom, I'm not sure I believe in this Catholic stuff… I don't think we eat the body and drink the blood of Christ." Max announced.

"Um… could we have this discussion later?" Morgan jerked her head toward Daisy who carefully selected chocolate chip cookies out of the box and placed them on a napkin.

"Oh, right. Sorry."

A dark-haired girl from class led Daisy away from the table to a far corner of the garden where they could eat the cookies without being bothered by the clutch of boys who chased each other among the saintly statues.

Morgan leaned over to Max and whispered in his ear, "If you don't believe in that, you probably shouldn't take communion. You can just cross yourself when you go up to the priest. You'll get a blessing and no one will know the difference. How's that?"

"Ok." Said Max. "You're not mad at me?"

"No, baby. I'm not mad at you. I'm impressed you actually thought about it. I don't think a lot of people do…" Morgan said as she pressed his head into her shoulder with a squeeze.

Later, Morgan watched as children dripped from the arms of their parents while they all pressed into each other's backsides in a rush to get to the priests standing at the steps of the altar. She hoped no one would notice if she casually crossed her arms just as she got to the priest at the front and bowed her head instead of getting a wafer pressed into her hands or placed on her tongue. She hoped Ben wouldn't notice. How would she answer the question if he asked?

Morgan did not have to take communion, but she had to go to confession. Even teachers who spent most of their time escorting kids to the toilet and handing out pencils had to go to confession to set an example for the children. It waited for her like a rabid housecat in the darkness.

"Morgan, hey. Sorry I haven't been in touch. Things have been crazy. I do want to see you but it's going to be a squeeze. Any chance you could have a late dinner with me tonight?"

Morgan again stood on the sidewalk in a deceptively bright London afternoon. It looked much warmer than it was. The breeze made dirt eddies around her feet.

"Ummmm… I can probably manage that. How late?"

"8:30?"

"Yikes, that's terrible timing. Where?" she asked.

"My hotel room?"

"Oh my God, I thought it was dinner."

"Well a guy can try, right?"

"I… I have a lot of questions…"

"Ok, ok…come to the lobby of the Intercontinental at 8:30 and I'll figure out a place for us to go eat."

"Ok. See you then. Bye."

"Bye beautiful. See you in a bit."

She pressed the red button on the phone to end the conversation and zombied her way through the rest of her day. School pick up. Homework. Dinner. She did battle with her lesser instincts and managed not to suck down a bottle of wine. The kids were most of the way into bed. Max read the latest Horrible Histories book as she kissed him on the forehead. Daisy's curly brown head nodded over her Fancy Nancy book. Morgan kissed her on the top of the head. The sitter would turn out the lights in a few minutes.

Jeff was not as tall as she remembered, but his presence filled the space around him. When he caught sight of Morgan, he grinned and put out his arm, swinging her into him as if closing a door. She did not look him directly in the eyes.

They walked out of the hotel and crossed the street. He asked where she wanted to go for dinner, but she had no interest in food. They walked toward Mayfair.

Jeff gave her a once over as they walked. "You've been falling apart."

"So much for hiding it," she thought. "No… not, not really," she stammered.

They arrived at a small Italian restaurant. Once again, flatterers appeared like mosquitoes at dusk. "Mr. Jeff, we're so happy to see you. Sit anywhere you like. We've missed you." "Mr. Jeff it has been too long, what are you drinking tonight?"

They sat opposite one another in a small booth. Jeff pulled out his phone and placed it on the table, then pressed her for decisions on the order. Morgan had no interest in eating, but managed to make a few choices that satisfied him.

When he wasn't on his phone, he pursued a line of questioning Torquemada would have been proud of. She struggled to stay upright as a wall of words fell on her like a tidal wave. Her inquisition chamber was a booth at a mediocre Italian restaurant, her arms pinned at her sides:

"What does your father do?", "I bet you were a Daddy's girl.", "How many siblings do you have?", "Have you lived anywhere else?", "How many kids do you have again?", "How old are they?", "I bet you are a good mom.", "What do you do for fun?", "What does your mother do?", What are your parents like?", "How long have you been married?", "Are you religious?", "What kind of music do you like?", "Where did you go to school?" Have you ever had an affair before?"

Despite her earlier bravado she was unable to give voice to the avalanche of questions in her own head: *"Did you really communicate with me telepathically?", "Can you do that anytime?", "Can you read my thoughts right now?", "Where did the vision of the accident come from?", "Can you explain the burned clothes?"*

But if he heard her thoughts, he chose to ignore them.

"You realize I get something like 1000 e-mails and texts a day." He said. "Everybody wants a shot at the big time. My priorities are work, my kids and then anything else." Morgan imagined she would be pretty far down the list if on it at all.

Between the main course and dessert he looked up into her eyes and made a statement as implausible as it was true, "I inflame your soul." It was a statement, not a question. There was nothing to say. Only more questions she was afraid to ask.

"When are you going to relax and start enjoying yourself?" he asked.

"That's difficult in the face of a tsunami."

He laughed. "I guess that's fair."

"You know what I really want to talk about… or I think you do."

A grin stalked her from across the table. "What do you want to ask me?"

"Did you really talk to me in my head?"

"Yeah. First I asked you to leave with me, but I had to do it three times, shit you're stubborn."

She should have expected that. Of course he would answer her in her head. But it still surprised her. *"How did you do that?"*

"I can't really explain it, it's just something I can do."

39

"But how can you make me hear you?" Morgan asked out loud.

"Not everyone can." As he spoke in her head, he looked as if he were pregnant with laughter; the grin got wider.

"And you can hear me?" she asked in her mind.

"Obviously." Now he gave birth to a few stunted chuckles.

"Can we please talk with regular voices? This is weirding me out."

"That's something I don't understand."

Morgan waved her hands in surrender. "Look, I'm losing my shit as it is now."

"Maybe you're not ready yet?"

"Ready for what?" asked Morgan.

"Me." He flagged down a waiter to order dessert and coffee and evade the subject.

"Please help me understand what's going on and how you're doing this?"

"As I told you, I don't exactly understand this ability that I have either. It's just something I can do. Everyone has different things they can do. Frankly, when I saw you in the restaurant I thought you were already aware. And usually the awake ones can communicate with me. Humans don't normally shine like that without awareness. That was bizarre and something I don't get."

"Awake ones?" She asked. Things were only getting worse.

"Oh God." His head went into his hands. He pressed the heels of his hands into his forehead. He rolled his head side to side as he said, "Wow. This has really never happened before. I think I better stop talking. Again, I ask, who the fuck are you??"

Tears stung Morgan's eyes. "I just want to understand what's going on. I've no idea what you're talking about and I don't know what to do. It's not just this. There's the thing with the wreck too. And my clothes."

"Your clothes?"

"The night I met you... all my clothes burned."

"Did your house catch on fire? What do you mean your clothes burned?"

Morgan sighed. "When I left I wished all my clothes would burn so... so... well, I don't know. But when I got back home, they had. The closet, even the rug was untouched. It was just the clothes. I have no idea what happened."

"Really? Are you sure about that? I don't actually believe that... maybe you are just pretending... again, who the fuck are you? And why aren't you telling me the truth?"

Morgan thought, *"I could say the same thing."* And then the storm of tears broke.

"Well, not exactly. But we need to get you out of here." The response from him came in her head.

"So he can hear my thoughts…"

"Only when I'm tuned into them. I'll try to explain. But we can't do it here."

Jeff asked for the check and wasted no time paying. As they rose from the table, he took her by the elbow and steered her out of the restaurant. The shock of the cold air stemmed her tears. When they got onto the street he put his arm around her shoulder. "Don't worry Morgan, you're going to be alright. In fact, so much more than alright. We need to go somewhere private to talk about this stuff. My hotel room is the best place. I promise not to try anything, ok?"

Morgan didn't agree or disagree, but she bummed a cigarette off of him to calm her nerves as they walked arm in arm. They hunched against the bitter cold of the London night past the American Embassy as they headed toward his hotel.

"Hey wait, I want to take you somewhere. My local is around the corner." Morgan had been around Brits long enough to know that when they call a bar their "local" it has special meaning to them, like a second home, but with all the alcohol you can drink.

"Uhh… I'm in no shape…"

"Oh you'll be fine, a drink will do you good. God knows I need one."

The security guard outside seemed to know him, but he did not get the obsequious attention she had seen elsewhere.

His local was a classic take on a London pub. A heavy oak counter with lots of brass and glass behind it stacked high with various bottles of alcohol. The room was paneled in dark wood. A crowd of people sat at four top tables squashed next to each other with the pub-perfume of fried food hanging in the air. She leaned against the bar as he again ordered five more drinks than they needed, and they talked about nothing until the cigarettes called to him again.

Morgan touched his arm as he started for the door pack in hand. "It's late, I need to get home soon."

"Ok. Let's go."

There was no more discussion, only an assumption that Morgan was headed back to the hotel with him. A big part of her wanted to jump into a taxi to escape from herself.

When they got upstairs, Morgan dropped into a chair at the far end of Jeff's hotel room. He went behind her to crack a window and produced a pack of cigarettes.

"Isn't this room…" she started to ask.

"Non-smoking. Fuck it." He said as he lit up a Marlboro Light and blew the smoke behind him toward the open window.

"So, try and tell me again how this 'ability' of yours works?" asked Morgan.

"I really don't know. I can just do it. I can tune into someone, and if they are on the same 'wavelength' or something - remember, I said not everyone is - they can hear me and I can hear them."

"And you thought I would be able to hear you when you saw me? Why'd you think that?'

"Because there are usually signs of people who would be able to hear me. I can see people who have shifted; they have a sort of shimmer about them."

"Like an aura?"

"Yeah."

"And my aura looks like that?"

"Yes."

"And what does that mean?"

He sighed and took another drag of his smoke, blowing a cloud out as he looked at the ceiling, "Usually it means that someone is already awake, that they know what their abilities are… that they understand that there is more to life than meets the eye."

"Lots of people understand that."

"Not in the same way. It's different and if you don't know it, you don't. It's hard to explain unless you've had an experience."

"Like seeing visions of accidents or communicating with strangers telepathically... or burning your clothes with a wish?"

"Usually it starts slower than that, at least with the people I've met. And usually you have some sort of mentor or a guru or something. Or you are trying to..."

"Are you my mentor?"

"No, I don't go in for that sort of thing. Again, it's not just that you had the shine... you're really pretty. And I..."

"Used telepathy to pick up on me?"

He laughed in response, "Yeah, I guess I did... but I thought you were in on the game so to speak."

"It's a game?"

"Shit. Don't take things so literally. Yes and no. All of life is a fucking game, this other shit just makes it a whole lot more interesting. I'm tired of talking about this right now. I need some space to think."

"Do you have a mentor?"

"Fuck no."

"So how'd you figure all this out?"

"Ummm... I'm different. I've known everything since I was born. I can't remember not knowing. But I've been betrayed by a lot of people, so I stay away from most of the awakened and I carefully control who I let in."

"What about me?"

"You sort of slipped in, and I'm not sure what to do about that yet. If you tell anyone about what has happened between us, you understand I'll deny it. I have too much at stake."

"I, I don't…" stammered Morgan.

"Sorry, sometimes I just get edgy… I don't like being well known." He stood up and held out his hand. She took it and almost snatched it away as his touch set off a peculiar but not unpleasant vibration she felt throughout her body. He gripped her hand and pulled her to her feet. He clasped one arm around her waist as he reached down and touched an iPad on the table making the screen come alive. He touched it again and music began to play. It was U2's, Stuck in a Moment.

"This is one of my favorite songs. Dance with me."

The frisson that echoed across her skin was renewed every time he touched her. Her skin felt like a pond touched by rain, each drop set off infinite ripples. When he cupped his hand around the back of her head, she felt a jolt like an electric shock. He bent down to kiss her.

*"I should not be doing this." S*he thought.

He started to laugh.

"Could you hear that?" she asked.

"I don't think I needed to, your body language was pretty obvious." He wrapped his arms around her and again she could feel herself yield to him like in the bar. She willed herself not to.

He stepped back and dropped his arms to his sides. "Look, I promised I wouldn't press you to do anything you're not comfortable with, and you don't seem very comfortable right now. Maybe you're not ready for me."

"What do you mean by that?"

"A whole lot of things that I'm not going to explain now. I'm tired, if you want to fool around please stay, if not, why don't you just take some time to figure out what you want to do."

Morgan sat in the chair and started to cry, "I have no idea…" She pressed her face into her hands, elbows on knees. "I don't understand any of this, or you."

Jeff sat down on the bed across from her. "I'm sorry. This is a little weird for me too and I don't know what to do about it either. It's probably better that we don't fool around right now. Why don't you go home and get some sleep… I bet you haven't had much lately. I'll be here for a couple of days and we can get together again before I go."

"And you'll try to explain this to me?"

"Yeah… I'll try to think of something…"

She stood up and moved to pass him. He grabbed her hand and kissed it. Then caught her eye, *"You have nothing to be afraid of, ever, not in this life or the next."*

He continued to hold her hand as he stood and clasped his mouth on hers. She felt herself going soft again. He held her face with both hands as their tongues found each other. An alarm sounded in Morgan's head. She smelled like cigarettes and cologne (her husband never wore it). She disengaged herself from his clasp and his ravenous mouth. His hands slid down her body and lingered on her rear.

"I love your ass. You have a great ass."

She wanted to slap him, but she held her hand and her tongue. He pulled her toward him again. This time he kissed her on the forehead and then looked into her eyes and said, "If you ever want to know anything about me, just look into my eyes. You will find everything you need to know there."

She turned toward the door as he continued, "Your best assets are your eyes and your smile. You should use your smile more often."

Day 8

The next morning she got a text from Jeff: Company crisis. Flying out today. Will be in touch.

Day 12

Morgan hovered outside of a tall apartment building. She knew it was Jeff's apartment (though he had never told her where he lived). She hung in the air before landing on the apartment balcony. Through the large window she could see white carpet and grey sofas facing a big screen TV. One wall held a red guitar mounted as though it were a precious painting.

Behind the living area, there appeared to be an open kitchen, with bedrooms down a hall that stretched beyond. It was clean, but not Spartan, comfortable, but not cluttered. At first she thought she had to open the door, but that was not necessary. She imagined herself in the room and there she was on the white carpet. She felt like an intruder and moved toward the wall near the kitchen so she wasn't standing in the center of the room. She had no idea if she could be seen. Near her was a doorway where light spilt out into the dark hall. A chair creaked.

Startled, she pressed herself against the wall and waited. As she settled into the quiet she heard the soft tap-tap of computer keys. It took some time to gather her courage and peek around the doorjamb into the room.

Jeff was seated at a large black table in front of a floor to ceiling window, his back to her as he hunched over his keyboard and stared at an enormous computer screen full of spreadsheets.

She watched as he leaned back in the chair until it squeaked in protest like a mouse was caught in the hinge. He stretched his arms over his head and cracked his knuckles, then cradled the back of his head with his intertwined fingers. She dared not stay and imagined herself back out into the inky night…

The yoga instructor's voice roused her from her daydream, "Wiggle your fingers and toes."

It took Morgan a moment to land back in the reality of dead body pose in the hot, smelly Bikram yoga room. Her clothes were so soaked through, she might as well have just stepped out of the shower. A bead of sweat traced its way down her neck and onto the double towel layer she had put on her mat.

The instructor continued, "Roll gently onto one side and pause." Morgan had not moved anything yet. She felt groggy and weighted. She concentrated on moving her extremities. Her toes and fingers responded and she pulled her knees up placing her feet on the ground before rolling to the side.

"Now come to a cross-legged position and rest for a moment." Morgan attempted to follow the instructor's direction but her limbs felt as though they moved through thick mud. Morgan got herself into the position with great effort and closed her eyes.

The class closed with a group "Om" and Morgan let the others pick up their belongings and leave the muggy room before she moved to get off her mat. Her mind contemplated the scene she just witnessed. She managed to drag herself to the changing room. Most of the others had already cleared out of the showers. She turned the spigot to cold and braced herself for impact in an attempt to shock herself awake and staunch the sweat so she could get dressed.

The cold air outside of the studio helped clear her mind as she walked down the alley to the street at Parson's Green. She picked up a couple of things at the grocery store on the corner and made her way to the tube stop. On the train she pulled her phone out to check for messages. There were two texts, one from Rachel and one from Jeff. She ignored the one from Rachel and opened Jeff's.

It was the first she had heard from Jeff since the cryptic message of departure. Not contacting him had tortured her over the last few days. Maybe he was ready to really talk and explain the telepathy, the weird visions and how she knew things she shouldn't know.

Jeff: Hey, was just thinking about you after wrapping up some work stuff. About to go to sleep. You around?

The message was 30 minutes old.

She texted back: On the tube. Can talk if you want.

Jeff: Feeling kinda horny. Wanna play?

Morgan flushed with anger, and then watched herself respond to his proposition while hating herself for doing it at the same time.

Morgan: Play? Play what?

Jeff: Haven't you ever had fun with texting?

Morgan: Fun? What do you mean?

Jeff: Jesus. Are you kidding? Have you never sexted before?

Morgan: No

Jeff: You're a nerd. Gorgeous. But a nerd.

Morgan: I have been married a long time.

Jeff: Yeah. I know. Kinda what I mean. Never mind. You killed the mood anyway.

Morgan felt a slight panic at his obvious disappointment. But at least she had his attention.

Morgan: Do you have a red guitar?

Jeff: ????

Morgan: Do you have a red guitar? On your wall? In your living room?

Jeff: What kind of game are you playing?

Morgan: I'm not playing a game.

Jeff: Have you been spying on me?

Morgan: No.

Jeff: Reading about me?

Morgan was not about to admit to the level of her obsession with him even if it had nothing to do with why she asked about the red guitar.

Morgan: No.

Jeff: No? Really?

Morgan: Nice ego.

Jeff: Ok. Then how do you know about the guitar?

Morgan: So you do have one?

Jeff: Yes, but you could know that from the band. It was my signature thing. The red guitar... I've had dozens of them.

Morgan: I don't remember that. But even if I did, how would I know that you have one on your wall like a work of art in your white living room?

Morgan was certain that this was the case, but she did not know how she knew that.

Jeff: Maybe you read about it somewhere.

Morgan: Has it been written about?

Jeff: I'm sure it is somewhere.

Morgan: Well, that's not how I know.

Jeff did not respond. The train stopped at Earl's Court Road. She put her bag on her shoulder and stepped off the train. Now she was pissed.

Morgan: And you know that.

Day 14

Morgan lay in bed. In the twilight between wake and sleep, she drifted. Jeff's voice echoed down to her as if she were in the bottom of a well.

"Get up, say nothing, meet me downstairs… you've been falling apart… I inflame your soul… if there's anything you ever want to know, just look into my eyes, you will see it there… if there's anything you ever want to know, just look into my eyes, you will see it there… if there's anything you want to know, just look into my eyes… if there's anything you want to know…"

She saw his sparkling blue eyes. The light in them danced like sun on a rippled pond, achingly clear and sharp. She fell in.

It was dark. She looked down and saw her feet, but they were not her feet. She wore socks with wooden sandals like the Geisha she saw in Japan. Why were her feet not on the ground? They dangled. She traveled up her body and saw a flowered blue kimono. She felt a pressure in her chest. It was hard to breathe.

Then she found herself in a Japanese style teahouse serving traditional tea. Plates and saucers of food lay on the table between her and the imposing man on the other side. He did not wear his helmet, but his katana was still strapped to his side. She recognised the regalia of a Samurai. His hard green eyes stared her down. His hulking figure was in deep contrast to the delicacy of the paper and bamboo walls decorated with watercolours of koi and cherry blossoms. In those eyes she recognised Jeff.

"You're mine," he said.

"I don't love you."

"The priest?"

"It doesn't matter."

"You know I can have you right now." He nodded his head in the direction of the sliding door behind him. "They won't stop me. They fear me too much."

"I'm not afraid of you."

"You should be." With that he lunged across the table and made a grab for her. As she reared back, her legs caught under her. The sound of breaking dishes heralded his move, china and food scattered everywhere in his wake.

He pressed a powerful arm across her chest to hold her down while he fumbled with himself. She struggled to pull her lower body out from under him. "There are rules…"

A full-mouthed laugh erupted from him, "What do I care for rules?"

"You are a Samurai…"

"A renegade Samurai…" the smile that crossed his face made her shudder as she felt his hands under her robes.

Morgan shifted and almost came fully awake but then found herself in a dark panelled room sparsely decorated. She wore a thin, pink, silk robe and lay on a futon. A man who wore the white robes of a temple priest came into the room. He took off the hat with the tails and placed it and the rest of his attire on a manikin in the corner. They could not touch the ground. He knelt on the futon next to her. *"This must be the priest…"*

She could see light just at the edge of the painted screen in front of the window. Cherry blossoms again. Next to it she could see white robes on a form, the black hat with the tails topping it off.

The door to the room slammed out with a loud crack. The enormous form of the warlord in full battle gear filled the space where the door had been.

"AAAAAAEEEEEEE" the man screamed as he raced to the futon, sword raised overhead. Morgan curled up and covered her head with her arms. There was no time to get away.

She heard the man next to her cry out, but it was cut short by the sound of a blade on flesh. She felt the warm spray on her body and heard the sound of something heavy hit the floor. She felt nothing. A blood covered torso lay next to her. His head was on the floor next to the bed. She was covered in blood. The bed soaked up the blood that poured from his severed neck. She turned to see the warlord at the foot of the bed. A slow smile spread across his face as he watched her take in the scene.

"I should have made you do it. But I'll let the priests take care of you." He turned and walked out.

Now she found herself in a town square surrounded by an angry mob. The mob shoved her toward a gibbet. She wore the flowered blue kimono. A wig was stuck on her head, but it was not hers. She knew she was not Geisha, but she did not know how she knew this. Then a word came to her in the dream. *"Miko… You are Miko…"*

She was on the dais in the center of the crowd now. A bag was put over her head. *"That's why it was dark in the beginning,"* she thought. She felt a jerk and realised they hung her… she saw her socked and sandaled feet dangling below her.

Morgan opened her eyes to the darkness. Her heart raced and her legs felt warm, ready to flee. Ben lay next to her snoring. She had no idea when he had come in. Her body felt as though a million tiny bubbles welled up within her. She was wide-awake now. She rolled over so as not to jostle the bed too much. She picked her computer up off the floor. The house was quiet except for the sound of Ben's nose. She tiptoed to the door and went downstairs. The new puppy sat at attention in her crate. No amount of stealth kept her from waking. Morgan let her out to pee and put her back in the crate. She went to the next room and curled up in her favorite chair cradling her computer.

She turned her phone on to play some music while she surfed the net.

She had a late night text from Rachel: Ugh. Can't sleep again. I need to get my yoga on again and get healthy. Please take me with you tomorrow. I know you must be going.

Day 15

The black cab pulled up outside her friend's elegant white and black townhouse just off Brompton Road. Rachel waited at the top of the steps. She snuffed out her cigarette on the rail and came down to the cab.

"Oh my God… how can you do that before a hot yoga class? I would die."

"Well, I'm going to die anyway, so what's one cig? I can detox that too."

"I can barely survive as it is."

Rachel turned and looked Morgan in the eye, "And how have you been surviving? What's been going on with you? You totally fell off the radar. You don't respond to my texts. I haven't seen or heard from you since the night we went to Nobu."

Morgan looked away, "Sorry, I've had a lot going on."

"Like what? Spill."

"Uhhhhh…"

"Parson's Green?" interrupted the driver.

"Yes, please." Morgan answered.

"What? Ben again? The kids? Are you really losing the ex-pat package? Maybe you could start with where you disappeared to after Nobu. I thought you were going to the bathroom and you never came back."

"I was really drunk that night. You guys seemed like you were having fun... I was feeling sick. You know sometimes when you have too much to drink and you just hit a wall. Time to go."

"Fun? We all had too much to drink. I'm so glad Deborah was there. I think she hit a wall too. I remember her suddenly standing up and telling me we were leaving. One of those guys may have pulled something. Anyway, we looked for you in the bathroom. We described you to the doorman. He said someone fitting your description left with a man."

"Oh, really?"

"If you don't feel like telling me that's fine. You know I love you. I don't care what you do. That jerk of a husband of yours sure isn't paying you any attention. I wouldn't blame you if you had a little fun with someone else."

"Well. Thanks."

"So did you leave with a man that night? Was it the grey-haired guy? The one who was kind of quiet?"

"Rachel."

"Right. Never mind. My lips are sealed. But if there's something about it that's bothering you, you really can talk to me."

Morgan inhaled deeply. "Ok. I did leave with that guy."

"The grey-haired one?"

"Yes."

"And then what?"

"We went to a bar and then we went home."

"Ok. So what's the big deal?"

"Well. We… uhhh… things have gotten a little weird. I don't know where to begin."

"Have you heard from him again?"

"Yes."

"Have you seen him again?"

"Yes."

"Oh wow."

"That's not the 'oh wow' part. We went to dinner and his hotel room, but I left and we didn't do anything other than kiss."

"So what's the 'oh wow' part?"

"You're going to think I'm nuts."

"Try me."

"Uhhhh…" Morgan inhaled again, "So the reason I left with him is because he asked me to without actually speaking."

"What do you mean? Did I miss a game of charades?"

"No. He talked to me in my head."

"What do you mean 'in your head'? How did he talk to you in your head?"

"Like telepathically."

"What? Are you sure you weren't just drunk?"

"I thought that too at first and then when the cab dropped him off at his hotel, he did it again. He told me his last name in my mind too. And then when we got back together for dinner and in his room we did it again… like a conversation but without words."

"Holy shit. Did you drink at dinner?"

"I had, like, a glass of wine. Not much. I was sober when we did it in his hotel room."

"You mean had a conversation in your heads?"

"Yes," Morgan sighed.

"Ok, honey this is crazy…"

"That's why I didn't want to tell you this stuff. I knew you'd think I was nuts."

"Ok, wait. We're not going to any stupid yoga class. I think we both need a drink. I know I do." Rachel tapped on the window behind the driver to get his attention. "Sir, sir…"

"Rachel, what are you doing?"

She laughed. "I'm telling him to turn round so we can go to Rules or something."

"We might know someone there. And we're in yoga clothes. Let's go to a pub somewhere."

The driver was now listening. "There's The White Horse on Parson's Green. We're almost there, you know, if you're wantin' a pub."

"Perfect. Please take us there," said Rachel.

They settled into a table for two in a back corner. Morgan scanned the place for anyone she knew, but saw no one.

"I'll go up and order, my treat," said Rachel.

"I don't really want anything to eat."

"Glass of white, anything but chardonnay, right?"

"Yep. That'll do it."

They chit-chatted until the wine came.

Rachel took a big sip and put her glass down. "Ok, please tell me again, in detail, what happened."

The noise of the pub fell away as the last two weeks gushed out of Morgan like someone opened floodgates. She told Rachel everything that had happened. How crazy she felt. How stupid. How guilty.

When Morgan finished, Rachel sat back in her chair and took another swig of her almost empty glass. "Do you remember when we met in Tokyo?"

"Yes, in the sandbox with Max and Madeline. I was pregnant with Daisy," answered a confused Morgan.

"How long ago was that? Eight years?"

"I think so."

"Do you know what I thought when I met you?"

"No."

"I thought; wow, this is one together woman. Here she is, pregnant, about to have a child in Tokyo, with a five-year-old in tow. She just moved here. You were funny and really grounded, and I liked you on sight. I knew we would be friends for a long time."

Morgan did not know how to respond, but tears welled in her eyes. She had felt really at sea when she moved to Tokyo, not grounded or funny.

"And here you are today, telling me this crazy story about telepathy and strange dreams and being psychic with some guy you hardly know. And the weird thing is, I don't feel any differently about you. If it were anyone else, I would doubt their sanity. But I can't. You are the sanest, most organized, on top of it person I know. You're not allowed to be crazy."

"Thanks… I think."

"No, seriously, I know people who have had psychotic breaks. You don't look like that. I don't know what's going on, but I don't think you're crazy."

"But what the hell do I do?"

A woman came to clear the glasses; both women smiled and handed them to her.

"I don't know, but let's try to think it through a bit. You met a man who talked to you in your head. And you think you burned your clothes up with a wish. And you've been having weird dreams where you see his apartment or where he's talking and things are happening to you? Right, is that everything?"

"Except for when I saw his kid in an accident."

"Oh right, and he told you that happened?"

"Yeah."

"And you believe you are right about seeing the apartment, but he didn't confirm that?"

"Right."

"Ok, this seems like the most bizarre conversation, but here goes. So it seems like the talking in your head... the telepathy is real, oh my God, and the psychic thing where you saw the wreck is real, and the dream or daydream where you saw his apartment is real, but that is sort of like psychic stuff, right?"

"Yeah, I guess so."

"So the things that are different are the burned clothes... and who knows, that could have been some freak electrical thing no one can figure out."

"Except that I specifically wished it would happen and Jeff got really mad when I mentioned it and thought I was lying to him about not knowing how I did it."

"Ok, have you talked to him about the dream?"

"Actually there were two dreams... but, no, I haven't had anything from him since the guitar question."

"Maybe you guys have some sort of weird connection or something. I don't know, but he needs to tell you."

"He keeps getting evasive when I bring stuff up… he just wants to talk sex."

"Did you look up Miko?" asked Rachel.

"Look up Miko?"

"You know, after your dream. I know what a Geisha is, but I've never heard of a Miko."

"I didn't think of that. That's a good idea. Rachel, thank you…"

"You don't need to say anything, this is what friends do. When I need help, who do I call? You. I'm just returning the favor babe. Whatever's going on, we'll figure it out." She got up and crossed the pub to the bar where she requested the bill.

Day 17

Morgan sat with the computer in her lap reading about celebrity plastic surgery gone wrong. Finally she took a deep breath and entered 'miko'. The first result was a Wikipedia entry. She clicked on that.

In Shinto, a Miko is a 'shrine maiden' or supplementary priestess. The Japanese word 'Miko' means 'female shaman'. In Japan these women were soothsayers, priests, magicians, shamans and prophets in the folk religion, and they were the chief performers in organized Shintoism.

Morgan stared at her computer. She reread the entry for 'Miko' on Wikipedia at least a dozen times. She noted that they were now reduced to receptionists and dancers at the temples - no more magic. A further note captured her attention:

During the feudal Kamakura period (1185-1333) when Japan was controlled by warring shogun states, the Miko were forced into a state of mendicancy as their shrines and temples went bankrupt. The traveling Miko known as 'aruki miko' became associated with prostitution. In the Meiji period many shamanistic practices were outlawed. There was an edict called the 'Miko Kandanrei' (1867), which was enforced by security forces loyal to the Emperor forbidding all spiritual practices of the Miko.

The effervescent feeling ran up Morgan's spine again. This was a dream she had. Or maybe it wasn't a dream. It felt like a long forgotten memory, stirred like dust on the floor of an abandoned house. She knew she had been a Miko who had an affair both with a warlord and a Shinto priest. The warlord found out and killed the priest, giving the rest of the priests in the temple the perfect excuse to try and execute her for murder. They had dressed her up as a Geisha and took her to another town because of her popularity. Morgan had no idea how she knew this, but she did.

"Mom have you seen my sports bag?" Max stood in the doorway of Morgan's bedroom.

"No sweetie. I hate to ask, but did you remember to bring it home from school?"

"Oh shit…" Max's eyes bloomed as he realized his mistake. "Sorry, mom, I think I may have left it on the bus. Can you call and see? If I get any more marks, I get a detention."

"Angel, is there any way to help you remember your stuff? There always seems to be something… a book, a bag, homework."

"Mom, I try, I really do…" Max's shoulders slumped. "Can you just call? Please?"

Morgan set her computer aside and reached for her phone.

Day 18

It had been five days since she had heard from Jeff. She felt like an unwatched pot about to boil over. The kids' rooms were now immaculate and devoid of any clothing that no longer fit them. She had paid every bill. There were no extraneous e-mails in her in-box. She had become obsessed with yoga.

She gave up.

Morgan: I really need to talk to you.

Jeff: In a meeting. Talk later.

Morgan wanted to scream. Or throw the phone. Or both. Daisy came into the kitchen.

"Mama, will you play a game with me?"

Morgan sighed. It was hard to switch gears. But she put on a smile. "Sure, sweetie, what do you want to play?" Even as she answered, she relaxed a bit. She hugged Daisy and kissed her on top of her head.

The little girl squeezed her quickly and ran into the family room. "I want to play Go Fish…" Daisy went into the cabinet and pulled out a pack of cards. She sat on the floor, dealt six cards each into two piles and placed the remainder of the deck in the middle. Morgan sat on the floor, facing Daisy.

"Ok, baby. You go first," suggested Morgan.

"Ask for an eight." A voice spoke in Morgan's head. It sounded like a child.

Morgan looked at Daisy, "Did you say something?"

"Not yet mama. Do you have a eight?" asked Daisy. Morgan took a deep breath and tried not to react. *"Did Daisy hear the same voice?"* thought Morgan as she nodded and pulled the card out of her hand to give Daisy.

"Now ask for a two." The voice was again in Morgan's head.

"Do you have a two?" asked Daisy.

Morgan handed another card to Daisy. It wasn't Daisy's voice in her head like Jeff; it was someone else.

"She doesn't have anything else you want right now."

"Hmmmm… well, I guess I have to go fish."

"You didn't ask me for a card."

"Oh sorry Mommy, do you have a Queen?"

"Go fish. But how did you know I didn't have a Queen before you asked?"

Daisy's eyes got wide. "Uhhhh… I just knew. I…"

"Can you hear a voice?"

"Ummmm… what voice?"

"Could you hear a voice telling you which cards of mine to ask for?"

"Ummm," Daisy looked at the floor. "Yes."

"It was a voice in your head?"

"Yes."

"Do you know whose voice it is?"

"Uhhhh… it's the little boy in pink knickers. I'm sorry Mommy, I thought it would make him happy… he seems so sad all the time."

"Wait, you mean your imaginary friend?"

"That's what you called him, but he was here when we moved in. Max used to see him too, but now he says he doesn't. I don't believe him."

"Wait a sec. You're telling me that you and Max see a little boy in pink knickers here in the house?"

"Yeah. He's a ghost."

"Your imaginary friend is a ghost? And you talk to him?"

"He seemed sad, so I asked if he'd like to play cards with us."

"You didn't deal him any cards?"

"No, Mommy, I don't think he can pick them up, but he knew your cards and told me which ones to ask for."

"So… you… were… getting him to help you cheat at cards?"

"Well, yeah, I guess. I just thought it would be a fun experiment and he seemed happy about it."

"Is he still here now?" asked Morgan as she looked around the room.

"No, he disappeared when we started talking about him. I guess he was embarrassed."

"So you can see him and hear him?"

"Yes. He comes to watch me play sometimes and I talk to him."

"What does he say to you?"

"He just tells me that he's sad and that he misses his mother. He doesn't say a lot. I think he's just lonely."

"Baby, will you let me know if he says anything else to you?"

"Ok, Mama. I will."

"And he doesn't scare you?"

"No, Mama, he's just a little boy."

"Are there any other ghosts around?"

"No."

"Have you seen any other ghosts?"

"Ummmm... yes. Is that bad?"

"No... no, I had a friend when I was a kid who had a couple of ghosts in her house. And she could see them." *"I was never sure I believed her,"* thought Morgan before she said, "What other ghosts have you seen?"

"I have seen the ghost of a woman at Pappy and Nana's house in New Orleans. There are lots of ghosts in New Orleans."

"Really? How come you didn't tell me before?"

"I don't know. I thought you might be scared."

74

"But you aren't scared?" asked Morgan.

"No, they're just ghosts. Most of them just seem lost, like they don't know where they're supposed to be."

"Ok, will you tell me if you see ghosts?"

"Did I do something bad?"

"No, baby, I think it's really cool that you can see them. I'm glad you told me… how long have you been seeing ghosts?"

"I've always seen them."

"Why didn't you tell me before?"

Daisy sighed, "I tried talking about it… you said it was my imaginary friend. It just seemed like no one else could see them, so I stopped talking about it. I didn't want anybody to think I was weird."

"Oh sweetheart… I'm sorry."

"It's ok Mama, you can't see them?"

"No, I can't see ghosts… but I could hear the little boy talking to you."

"That's funny… that must be really strange."

Morgan laughed, "It is a little. But what was funnier was that I realized YOU could hear him too. That's kind of cool."

"Maybe you'll be able to see them sometime too."

"Maybe," said Morgan.

"Do you think I'm weird?"

"No, baby, I think it's very sweet that you want to make him feel better."

"I just hate to see him so sad… do you want to keep playing?"

Morgan nodded her head, "Sure, was it my turn?"

Day 19

Morgan's desire to understand the mounting inexplicable events beat out any concern she had about looking desperate to Jeff. Another day had passed and "later" for talking had never come. She texted him again.

Morgan: I need to talk to you, please call me.

Jeff: In a meeting. Will call in an hour.

Two hours later her phone rang.

"I've got about five minutes, you got something else about one of my kids?"

"No, not this time."

"I don't have a lot of time. Shoot."

"So, unusual stuff is continuing to happen, like the other night I had a weird dream and you were in it… and there was another dream before that…"

"Oh, now we're getting somewhere; was it hot? What were we doing?"

"We didn't look like ourselves. You were a Samurai or something and I was dressed up as a Geisha except I wasn't a Geisha… I was a Miko or something…"

"Costumes? Now we're talking. I can do role play if it goes somewhere good."

"No, in both dreams you raped me. We didn't look like ourselves, but I knew it was you…"

"I'm sure it was nothing. Just a dream."

"Jeff I'm losing it over here. Please, please help me or give me some idea of how to get help."

"Ok, look, it sounds like a past life."

"A past life?"

There was a deep sigh on the other end of the phone. "Yeah, a past life. I don't really want to get into all this with you, but clearly we've known each other before. There's a connection between us. And I really don't wanna talk about it because every time we see each other or talk or text the connection just gets stronger and more shit is going to come in and you're going to see more and more about me and that is exactly what I don't want."

Before Morgan could respond the phone went dead. She called Rachel.

"He just hung up on me."

"Who? Jeff?"

"Yeah, I finally got him to call and he hung up on me. He told me the dream was a past life. He told me that we have a connection. He doesn't want to have the connection because I'll see stuff about him and he doesn't want that."

"Wow. Ok. Asshole. What now?"

"I have no idea."

Day 21

Morgan got home from the school walk and went upstairs to her bedroom. The computer waited for her. She opened her e-mail and found a note from Jeff.

Morgan,

I'm sorry I lost my temper the other day. I know you don't understand what's going on, but this is just really, really hard for me. I have been through some bad shit. So bad that I don't talk to my parents or my siblings anymore. Almost everyone I have ever known and trusted has betrayed me. I trust no one. Yes, I have been avoiding you because the connection between us will only get stronger the more contact we have. The stronger it gets, the more you will be able to see about me. And I am not ok with that.

I'm sure the dream was a past life. Now that you have tapped into some of your past lives, you will probably continue to see more past lives that are relevant to you, maybe in your dreams, maybe in other ways. I can offer this piece of advice - look up Carl Jung and spirit guides unless you already know about this. We all have spirit guides. I can't believe you aren't talking to yours yet. You're certainly at a level where you should be able to talk to them. Maybe reading about it will help you get there. Don't take this personally. You seem like a nice person and once you figure out who you are and what you can do, things will be very different. I just can't be the one to help you do that. The risks are too high for me.

Jeff

Day 22

She had not been terribly successful at adultery. In the Catholic Church even contemplating adultery is a sin and she had kissed another man and done a lot of contemplating. Jeff was not going to explain the crazy stuff to her. Should she confess the telepathy, the psychic visions, the burned clothes? What would the priest think? But if she did go to confession maybe the visions and dreams would stop, maybe she could get her old life back. Maybe she could get her hijacked mind back.

St. Mary's was a beautiful old stone pile in the heart of Chelsea. The heavy wooden doors gave way to an animated airy space covered by vaulted and veined ceilings. Long dark pews lined the inside with a center aisle leading forward to a gold cross, suspended over the steps to the altar. On the enormous crucifix was a painting of Christ as victim and robed in the red majesty of a god. St. Mary's was a place where hundreds of thousands of prayers and the smell of incense were so embedded in the walls that they could no longer be washed away.

The confessional was built into the wall at the back of the church near the gold-capped baptismal font. Two wooden doors with a light above were all that marked the space. The door on the right led to the priest's cabinet where he sat to hear confessions. The door to the left was for the supplicant. Morgan sank down into a nearby pew to wait for the light to turn green, indicating the cabinet was free. Tears slid down her cheeks. She begged God to help her.

Finally the door opened and a man stepped into a pew near the front of the church to pray. She opened the door and knelt down in front of the screen.

She crossed her forehead, heart and shoulders as she said, "Forgive me Father, for I have sinned."

"In the name of the Father, the Son and the Holy Ghost, I pray you will make a full confession."

"Uhhhh... well... I have lied and uhhh... I haven't been as kind and patient with my children as I should be... and uhhh.... I have not been a very good wiiiiiiffffe..." She sobbed, she heaved sighs and hiccupped tears. "I... have... comm... itted... ad... ul... tery... or... I al... most did... I want to... and... I... don't... know... what... to... do... I,I,I don't... even... know... if... I... be... lieve... in... any... thing... any... more."

"This is a really brave thing you have done coming here today. Not many people would have the courage to do this and be really honest. This took a lot of nerve," said the priest.

Morgan whimpered. Kindness, like light, emanated from behind the screen.

The priest continued, "You sound so miserable. It sounds to me like your foot is nailed to the floor and you're just flailing around. What's keeping it there? I think you need to go back and ask God to show you how much he loves you. He would not want you to be in agony."

She used most of the tissues in the box at her elbow. The priest suggested that she use three prayers: ask God to show her how much he loves her, ask Him to have mercy on her, and ask him for guidance. She slipped out of the box and poured what was left of herself into a pew. Another supplicant encased himself in the box as she tried to pray.

She returned home, curled up in her favorite chair and downloaded defiant music. She called every friend she could think of to arrange coffee or lunch. She did a lot of yoga. She tried to fill every moment with frenzied activity. Jeff may not have consumed her every moment, but he was just around every corner.

Day 23

Morgan picked up the phone to call Rachel.

"Hey kiddo. What's going on in psychic world over there?"

"I got an email from Jeff."

"I hope he apologized."

"He did, but then he said that he can't help me. He doesn't want to see or talk to me either."

"Why the hell not?"

"Because he's afraid that I will know more things about him, and he doesn't trust anyone. It sounds like he's scared of me."

"Freak. That pisses me off."

"I think I told you, he said the dream was a past life and said I might see others. He also said I should look up Carl Jung and spirit guides. He seems to think I should be able to talk to spirit guides."

"Past lives and spirit guides... are you serious? Maybe he's just crazy."

"Ugh. I would like to think so, but I don't. Too many strange things happening."

"Ok, I just googled spirit guides... do you have your computer nearby?"

"Yeah, it's right here," said Morgan.

"Do that, google 'spirit guides'."

Morgan entered the term in the search bar. The first thing that came up was entitled '4 Ways to Connect With Your Spirit Guides'. Morgan started to scan the article. Her phone spoke.

"Hey yoohoo, Morgan, I'm still here."

"Oh gosh Rachel, I'm sorry I put you on speaker and then forgot about you looking at this thing."

"It's ok. Go read it and tell me what happens."

"Thanks honey, will do. Bye."

Morgan went back to the search results and opened several different articles: '11 Ways to Connect With Your Spirit Guides', 'The 5 Types of Spirit Guides and How to Talk to Them', 'How to Talk to Your Spirit Guides', 'Your Guide to Your Spirit Guides', 'Befriend Your Spirit Guide', Spirit Guides magazine. There were 2,390,000 results for her search.

"Jesus, you've got to be kidding me," thought Morgan, *"this can't be how you connect with a spirit guide."*

"You got any better ideas?" A voice spoke in her head.

"Uh… excuse me…" She looked around to see if Rowena had spoken to her from the kitchen. No one was there. She caught her computer as it started to slide off of her lap, "Who's this?"

"Your spirit guide, who else? And may I say, it's about fucking time."

"I'm sorry, 'fucking time'?"

"We've been trying to get your attention for a while now."

"Ok, but you don't sound much like a spirit guide."

"What, you wanted a guide who sounded more like...?"

"I don't know, someone who sounded more like God or something."

"You have a mouth like a sailor on a three-day binge. I am only a reflection of you. You need someone you can relate to."

"And I can relate to you?"

"Hopefully, otherwise what's the point?"

"And what is the point?" asked Morgan.

"Ultimately the point is for you to learn to follow your heart. Just like that lovely psychologist told you sooooo many years ago. Your biggest problem is that you think too damn much."

"And you're going to help me think less?"

"Yes. And to pay attention to your heart more."

"Why are you talking to me now?"

"I have always been talking to you, you just didn't know it was me. Maybe you thought you were talking to

yourself. Maybe you passed it off as a gut feeling. Do you remember hearing my voice when you were a kid?"

"You played the movies. My imaginary friends?"

"That's what your mom called me and the others."

"Why did you go away?"

"We didn't. You just stopped listening to us. Your mind got cluttered with distractions in the material world: your life, boys, school, your husband, your kids."

"So what changed?"

"Your mind got less cluttered because you hated your thighs."

"What?"

"You did all that hot yoga because you wanted thinner thighs, you accidentally got a quieter mind and then 'le voila', you can hear us again."

"What do you mean 'a quieter mind'?"

"You stopped listening to the bullshit in your head. You tuned in. It's why you can now hear Daisy's ghost boy and Jeff."

"So what's the difference between you and Daisy's ghost?"

"'Ghosts' as you call them, want you to do something for them. Spirit guides do something for you."

"Ok, so what are you doing for me?"

"Guiding you, helping you move forward, helping you learn to follow your heart, that sort of thing."

"And Jeff?"

"Let's say it was a conspiracy on this side of reality to get you two back together."

"Back together?"

"You have known him before."

"So you mean all of this shit is real?"

"Yes."

"So does that mean Jeff and I are meant to be together?"

"Not necessarily. It can be different in each life. You have to figure out what is meant to happen in this life; not all soul mates are meant to last, some are just lessons."

"You can't just tell me?"

"Nope. I can guide you, not do for you."

"Uhhh... ok. Do you have a name? What should I call you?"

"Names and gender are irrelevant to us. But if you need a name you can call me Ariadne."

"Ok Ariadne, what do we do now?

"You ask for my help when you need it."

"Anytime? For anything?"

"Yes. Anytime, for anything."

"So what should I do now?"

"Learn something about Carl Jung and see what he has to say about spirit guides."

"Why don't you just tell me?"

"Because you need to do the work. Again, I just 'guide' you. You have to make your own decisions and choices. I just help you. Think of it like a game; it's a treasure hunt and I am giving you the clues."

"And when I find the treasure?"

"You know who you are and what you were sent here to do."

"That would take a fucking miracle at this point," said Morgan.

"Exactly. So get cracking."

Morgan became aware that she had been in the same position for a long time. She stretched and her stomach growled. Downstairs in the kitchen she saw that she had also forgotten to let the puppy out for playtime. She let her out of the crate and ushered her toward the back door. Morgan fished in the fridge and found some leftover curry that she put on a plate and stuck in the microwave. Retrieving her computer from upstairs she returned to the kitchen to let the puppy back in. Gertie went straight to her toy basket and snuffled a squeaky monkey out of the bottom. The toy burped wheezing squeaks with her attempts to get a better hold on it with her mouth.

"Good girl. Sit. Now give the toy to Mommy. Give the toy to Mommy."

The dog pulled back to play tug-of-war. Morgan dropped the toy.

"Gertie, sit."

The dog finally sat and released the toy so Morgan could play fetch with her. After 10 minutes the dog lay down with the toy and did not return for Morgan to throw it. Morgan then offered her a chewy in exchange for the toy. Morgan took her computer and moved into the den, flopping into her favorite chair. The puppy followed with her chewy and settled at Morgan's feet.

Opening the computer she entered 'Carl Jung Spirit Guides' in the search bar. The first snippet that came up on the Internet caught her attention:

Jung received his book, 'Seven Sermons to the Dead' through what he called automatic writing. "The start of the process of 'receiving' the book over a three-day period was like a 'possession'. Jung had spirit guides, one of whom was named Philemon. 'Philemon represented a force outside of myself which said things I had not consciously thought,' stated Jung."

"Oh great," thought Morgan.

Then she noticed another entry, "Jung's spirit guide was, in fact, a demon in disguise who led him into darkness." She clicked on that thumbnail and read more of the article.

"Uhhhh... Ariadne?"

Silence. Maybe it had all been her imagination.

"Ariadne, can you help me?" Morgan asked again in mind-speak.

"Well done! You asked." Replied Ariadne

"Is this supposed to make me feel better, that Carl Jung had a spirit guide who may have been a demon?"

"Does it not?"

"I'm not so thrilled about the demon part."

"Do I feel like a demon to you?"

"No, talking to you gives me a warm reassured feeling." Morgan noted a tranquil sensation like a furry cat taking a nap on her chest when she spoke with Ariadne.

"So I don't feel like a demon?"

"No. But what do I know? How do I know you're not a demon? Maybe you're being sweet to lure me in."

"Demons feed off of negative energy, they are the servants of Fear. But this does not make them 'evil' in the way that many perceive it. They are as necessary to the Universe as rain is to the earth."

"Are you telling me demons are a good thing?"

"There is no good and bad in my realm, these are only labels that humans applied to have a sense of control or understanding and instead it has led to terrible confusion."

"Ok. But what do I do if a demon shows up?"

"Offer it your heart and it will be tamed."

91

"Isn't that like a recipe for possession?"

"No. You need to learn to see signs, how to follow your heart and not your head and to forget everything you think you know. Then there will be nothing that you cannot do, even deal with demons."

"Shit. I sure hope you're not planning to test me on that one."

Ariadne laughed in response, *"All in good time my friend. You need a bit more training first."*

"Training? Is that what this is?"

"Yes, actually. You need to start writing down all of your experiences, starting with meeting Jeff. And I'm going to introduce you to some muses to help you."

"Muses? Are you serious?"

"You just pick up your computer and start writing. They will come."

Morgan placed the computer in her lap, fingers poised over the keys. Voices exploded in her head, *"We are your muses and we are here to help you write!"* Three green, M&M shaped creatures with spindly legs and arms appeared, standing at attention in the middle of her living room. They were knee high with round cow eyes.

"Uhhhh... ok, sorry?" Morgan could not help smiling. They were the kind of creature that just made you want to smile. They seemed so earnest and so ridiculous at the same time.

"We are here to help you write!" This statement was accompanied by serial backflips after which they chased each other in circles.

"I have always wanted to write, but I never could figure out what..." thought Morgan. She feared being dizzy if she watched them too long. She closed her eyes. Maybe she was dreaming. She opened them again. They were still there. Her mind spun like the green whirling dervishes dancing on the rug near the now sleeping dog. Maybe she was hallucinating.

"That... is... why... we... are... here..." Staccato style, one, two, three, they spoke in turn.

"You don't look much like Muses."

They halted so fast they ran into each other Three-Stooges style. They turned toward her, *"You don't like us?"* Wide mooneyes looked at Morgan from shiny green skin. If their round bodies contained shoulders they would have drooped.

"Oh no, you're lovely and very entertaining, you just don't look like the classic muse. You know, a beautiful woman holding some sort of musical instrument?" said Morgan in mind-speak.

The muses grew long blonde hair and fat red lips where no mouths had been before. They minced around the room and Morgan noticed high glittery heels on their skinny feet.

Morgan thought, *"Oh my God, are they playing dress-up?"*

They collapsed in a giggling heap. *"Is that better? Hahahahahahahahaha."*

"Okay, okay, what are we going to do?" Morgan asked.

"We are going to help you wrrrrrriiiiiittttteeee..." tumbling, somersaulting, they never seemed to stop moving.

"Okay, how are you going to help me write?"

"Don't you know? We are your inspiration!!!" They cartwheeled in sync across the floor. *"You have your computer. Just start writing. Seeeeeeeeeeee... we already helped youuuuuuuuuu."* They took turns, talking in sequence.

Morgan could not help laughing. She tried hard not to question how effective they might be.

"Just start typing... there will be a story for yooooouuuuuuu..." The muses leapfrogged across the room.

"Do you all have names?"

They stood at attention. *"Do we need them?"* The muses asked in unison.

"I don't know. You don't have individual names?"

They stood in a line looking at one another and shaking their heads, except they did not have heads separate from their bodies, so it was more like a whole body shake. *"No, do you need us to? We love you and we will do anything we can for you. Do you want us to have names too?"*

"Are you just the 'muses'?"

Yeeeeeessssss…we love you! Now start writing!" They bounced like balloons.

Morgan laughed. *"But what am I supposed to write about?"*

"Trust us! We will take care of that. You just start typing." In an instant they jumped on the back of the chair and leaned forward over her shoulders to stare with great anticipation at the blank computer screen.

"Uhhh… ok…. I'm not really used to having an audience."

"We. Are. Helping."

"How do I know what to write?"

"We play the movie in your head… you start writing. Wheeeeeeeee…" They cartwheeled off the chair.

Morgan stared at her computer screen uncertain, but as she typed, scenes emerged in her head. Her fingers moved as fast as they could to keep up with the images flashing through her mind.

"Yayyyyyyyyyyyyyy! We are going to write! We love you!!!"

The sand that seeped into her sandals burned her feet. The midday sun beat down, a golden disc in the sky raining heat and light with such intensity creatures with the choice stayed in shadow. She trudged on. She had to get to the place in the desert outside of town before the rest of the wizards. No one else would be out in the heat this time of day. It was the only time to go even if she had to wait for hours once she arrived.

The rush of the last year pressed itself upon her like the heat. She was on an errand for the Queen; a quixotic-tempered Queen she feared more than loved. A worm of concern for her mentor Mephistopheles squirmed in the back of her mind, but if he had betrayed the Queen then there was no going back. His fate was not for her to decide. The Queen told her that the wizards kept women (and girls) from the true knowledge. What was the point of that?

The hot breath of the wind ruffled her hair and danced around her shoulders. Cassandra smiled at the caress. It was as though the wind was her lover and confidant. The sacred caves were ahead. There was a secret entrance to the chamber and the place of meeting but she would have to wait and see where that was as she did not yet know.

A cave yawned from the wall of rock. She crawled inside and out of sight; she was small enough to conceal herself. Hours passed and her legs began to ache no matter how she shifted them. Her water ran low, but it would not be long now. The sudden darkness of the desert fell. The men would come soon.

A full moon shone on men riding camels on the flat desert below. They came in silence up the road, a group of twelve. She recognized Mephistopheles, the Royal Alchemist and his assistants. Their camels knelt on the moon-shadowed road next to the rocky outcropping. The men dismounted. She held her breath in the shadows of the cave. Wizards, how could they not know she was there?

A voice came into her mind, *"you are protected. Another whom you do not know watches over you and your errand."*

The wind kicked mini sand storms in the road. The men hurried to a single rock on the edge of the dune and disappeared. How had they done that? What trick had she missed? Damn these wizards, the Queen would be furious with her.

Cassandra crawled to the mouth of the cave and peered into the moonlit darkness. A breeze kissed her forehead and played with her hair.

Unattended, the camels shifted from foot to foot looking bored but showing no inclination to go anywhere. One rocked to his back heels and lowered himself like an awkward duck to the ground. The rest followed as if directed. The musky scent of camel joined the heat as it cast itself from the ground to meet the cool of the night descending.

She smiled to herself as she crept over to the rock where the men had disappeared. There was no obvious entrance. As she wondered if some incantation was required to enter, the ground swallowed her up from beneath. It was like falling in a dream and then finding yourself awake. Confused and breathless she arrived in a heap on a hard dirt floor. The sorcerers stood around her in a circle, laughing.

"Oh, my favorite mischievous little one, what have you done now?" Mephistopheles leaned over to help her stand. He smiled at her as if he knew every secret she had ever kept. "You did not really think that you could hide from me, did you?"

What could she say? She turned red and looked at the ground. It was like being naked in the company of everyone she ever knew.

He continued to tease her while the others looked concerned. "Little raven, don't you think I could have hidden this place from you if I chose to do so?" He turned to address the rest of the group, "She is an unwitting pawn of forces that she does not yet understand and she does not even know whose pawn she is."

Alcamar, who had never been her favorite, said, "Phisto, this is not a game. The book is not a toy. The Queen cannot have it."

"Everything that happens is written in the sands of time. We are written and erased and as small as any one grain of sand. What will be, will be," said Mephistopheles as he held Cassandra's gaze.

"We should kill her now." A voice barked from behind her.

"You will do nothing of kind. If anyone moves to hurt this child, he will answer to me." Phisto's voice had the low rumble of distant thunder. "She is doing exactly what she should, what I want her to do and that is why no one will touch her. I want her to know that I hold nothing but love for her."

Now Cassandra became weak. She felt nauseated; no longer defiant or powerful. But there were no more choices. "Where is the book?"

"My love, it is here. And I wish you to take it. These men will do nothing to stop you." His large hand reached out to pet her and then he kissed the top of her head. His mouth hovered over her, "You have learned well. And the price you pay will be no less than mine, but you will be ready and you will take revenge for both of us when the time comes." He whispered into her hair.

She could no longer see for the tears that crowded her eyes. He pressed a heavy, oversized book into her hands and when she did not respond, he opened her arms and pulled them across the book so as to hug it against her chest. She did not resist.

"Mephistopheles, you have betrayed us." Alcamar again.

"No more than you have betrayed yourselves. Why did you seek the power of the book? Were your reasons more pure than the Queen's? No, I can see inside your hearts. The book will not remain long in the Queen's hands. Trust me. All will be as it should."

"But what about us? What is to become of us?"

Phisto laughed, "Well you can take your chances out in the desert or ride back to Alexandria with me and into the keeping of the Queen's guard. You are likely to die either way."

"You mean you are going to take this child back to the Queen with the Book and just give them to her knowing your own fate?"

"We all die. I have known my fate for a long time. It is a small thing."

"I for one am not going to just-" the man's words were cut off as his clothes dropped to the ground like forgotten laundry. No bones. No blood. Nothing but a heap of dust. Mephistopheles was elegant even in killing.

"Anyone else?" Phisto's eyes made the rounds, challenging any of the men to make a similar move.

Cassandra tried not to drop to the ground herself. She must have realized what the endgame would be. How could she have thought it would be any different?

Mephistopheles put his arm around Cassandra's shoulders and guided her forward. "You will ride with me, I don't trust any of them."

He led her to his camel still kneeling with the group in the moonlight. They mounted in silence and the camel rose from his position and carried them toward the city. Several of the men turned away into the desert. Phisto said nothing and let fate take them. The rest followed their leader hoping he had a secret plan.

As they rode Mephistopheles whispered into her ear, "I love you Cassandra. I love you as the daughter I never had. You are a powerful sorceress, never forget that. Whatever happens to me, remember I could stop it. I could change things, but I will not because when you are truly powerful, you understand the beauty of fate and the beauty of the world the way it is. You must understand this and not blame yourself for all that is to come. I see ahead and I know what is to come. I have no fear; I welcome each moment like a lover. You have done everything right. I am proud of you, I love you. I love you. I love you."

He repeated these things to her like a spell all the way to Alexandria where the Queen's guard greeted them at the city gate.

The camels stood at attention, bemused by the torches in the darkness. The smell of camel mingled with the cold sweat of the men in front of them.

"Mephistopheles, you are under arrest for high treason." The Captain moved toward the lead camel with Morgan and her mentor.

Mephistopheles leaned down to kiss her on the crown of her head.

The camel knelt on its front knees and Cassandra allowed the guards who now surrounded them to remove her. A soldier tried to pry the book away from her now aching arms, but she refused. So they simply lifted her off. It was the last time she saw Mephistopheles alive.

A scuffling noise wrenched Morgan out of Egypt. The puppy sniffed the spot in front of her on the rug and started to squat.

"Oh no, no, no, no..." Morgan jumped up and tossed her computer on the sofa next to the chair. She scooped up the wriggling, confused creature just as a warm stream of pungent pee started from her backside. "Oh shit." Morgan ran through the kitchen, wrenched open the door to the patio and dropped the puppy to the ground. She started wagging her tail and barking. Gertie thought they were playing a game. Morgan slammed the door. "Ugh," she grunted as she headed up the stairs to change.

When she got back to the kitchen, Rowena was mopping the floor, "Oh God, thanks Rowena. I was about to do that. She peed all over me and I had to change first."

Rowena stifled a giggle, "It's fine Ma'am. Do you want me to let her in now?"

"We need to mop the floor with the stuff that kills the smell of pee or she'll keep doing it inside." Morgan retrieved the odor killing liquid from under the sink.

"I'll do it Ma'am."

"Ok, thanks."

Morgan returned to the den and sat back in the chair. The three muses had been sitting on the sofa until Morgan returned to the room.

"Yayyyy, we are going to write!"

"So I just keep going?"

"Yes! We will help you." They bounced up and down like children eager for a turn on a swing.

Morgan smiled and picked up her computer. The movie channel in her head continued.

105

"Cassandra, you have the book! You have done well my lovely....I love you so much, we are going to be so very happy. Have you looked at it yet?" asked the Queen. The ministers surrounding her looked frustrated by the interruption, but they said nothing.

Cassandra was smart enough to know that this was a trick. The Queen would have been furious if she had taken a peek at the book before her royal highness got a chance to see it. With a wave of the Queen's hand the men and the maids scattered into the curtains and the darkness at the edges of the room like annoying flies.

Cassandra walked straight to her and held the book out in both hands. The Queen cackled with delight.

"This is what I have been waiting for. There is no enemy who will be able to touch me once we have learned the secrets of this book you and I."

"You're a sorceress too, so why do you need me?"

"What I can do has been hard won, I do not have the natural skill that you do. Mephistopheles told me about you when you were still a child, practically a babe in arms. You can will things to happen, and I don't have that kind of power. I have to work at it, but you seem to hold the secrets of the Universe even if you don't know it."

Cassandra looked at her.

She continued, "But I can only imagine what you will be able to accomplish once you have learned the secrets in this book. You and I together."

Cassandra wept.

"You are sad for Phisto aren't you? He was a despicable traitor who would not help me. I know you were close to him, so I will allow you your tears for now. But mark me, traitors are no friends of mine."

She ran her hands over the book like a new lover. She pulled at the cover as if to open it, but nothing happened. It would not open.

She looked at Cassandra. Cassandra stared wide-eyed at the unyielding book as the Queen tried to pry it open. No luck. She took it off of her lap and put it on the bench beside her.

"Why can't I-" And then she sat back and smiled to herself. "Ahhh, of course, not just anyone can open this book. There must be a secret..." She turned to Cassandra again and asked, "Did you see them put any spells on it or use an incantation to open it up?"

"I never saw them use it. Phisto just handed it to me when I materialized in the cave. I was in the middle of their circle and he just handed it to me. I've held it tight ever since."

"Why don't you try?" The Queen edged away from the oversized volume. Cassandra stepped forward and reached her hand toward the book. She had not noticed anything weird about it since Phisto placed it in her grasp. Now touching the cover caused the tiny hairs on her arm to stand up in anticipation. As she pulled her hand away the book opened to reveal a glittering script in a language Cassandra had never seen. It sparkled and danced on the page as if lit by sunlight from within.

"What is it? What do you see?" Asked the Queen.

Cassandra was confused. "You mean you can't see this?"

"No, see what?" asked the Queen.

Casssandra opened the book further as the script moved like a living force as if written by an unseen hand.

The Queen looked from the book to Cassandra and back again.

"What do you see?"

"I see writing in a script that is unfamiliar to me."

"Let me look, I know more languages than you. It may be Greek, you don't know Greek do you?"

"No, but-"

The Queen snatched the book away from Cassandra, but as she took it, the cover snapped shut, surprising them both.

"What did you do?"

"Nothing."

"Ahhhh, perhaps only one person can see the book at a time. I know Phisto was the only one with access to it. Maybe *that* is the way it works. Give it to me."

"What?"

"Give it to me. Give me the book just like Phisto did for you. Give it to me the exact same way he gave it to you."

Cassandra picked the tome up off the bench with both hands and presented it to the Queen. The Queen grabbed it out of her hands and again tried to open it. Nothing happened. She threw the book on the floor and jumped up with fists clenched.

"AHHHHHHHHH..." She screamed without words. Ministers peeked out from behind the folds of curtains and quickly put their heads back into their quivering shells. As shrill screams reverberated off of the marble covered room, the Queen ran from table to table swiping them clean with her angry arms. The crashing, tinkling and shattering of earthenware filled the space. She threw a bottle of perfumed oil to the floor. The sound had a smell now;

the pungent heavy odor of harum filled the hall like invisible smoke.

Cassandra stood still, an oasis in the chaos.

The Queen collapsed heaving on her white curtained bed of goose down. She clutched the sheets and shredded them with her bare hands. Her rage refueled, she searched the rubble she had created in her anger. Finding a knife she returned to the bed and stabbed it with the ferocious desire of a kill.

"Uhhhhhh! Ah!" animal sounds were perforated with unintelligible screams.

Cassandra waited.

The force of the tantrum was so great even her wig had shifted, so her face looked lopsided.

"GEEEETTTTT OOUUUUUUTTTTT. All of you! OUT. NOW. Every one of you!"

She tore the curtains from the walls and revealed the men cowering behind them. She came at one with the knife raised, but he rolled away just in time as she turned to give chase to her prey. The remaining men took advantage of her hunt and scurried for the door on the other side of the room. A door slammed, speaking to the safety of some. But the little fat map man took too long to reach his destination, making him an easy target for the Queen's rage. She was on a blood hunt now. Someone had to pay because the book would not cooperate.

She raised the knife as she closed in on him. He could hear her behind him, as the guttural sounds got closer. He turned too late to defend himself. The Queen plunged the knife down into his back.

He collapsed sideways. She fell on him in a frenzied stabbing cyclone.

"Please! Stop. No! NO. Please." The pleas were punctuated by screams of agony.

Cassandra closed her eyes.

The sounds stopped. The man stopped writhing as the blood poured out of his body, running across the floor as if it too sought shelter from the attack.

The Queen knelt in the midst of the crimson pool, her white dress soaked in it. Her hands dripped. "Ah. Ah-hah." She exhaled and sat back on her knees.

Dropping the knife into the sticky mess she said, "I never liked that man anyway. Useless." She exhaled again and took in the scene around her. Everything in the room was as broken and bloodless as the man before her. "What a mess." Placing her hands on the ground in front of her, she played in the pooled blood as though it were a puddle on a summer's day. "To think we are made of this... this sticky stuff." Her hand dripped with it; she went to stand up and collapsed back down.

Cassandra took a step toward her as if to help her rise. The Queen shot her a look. She stepped back.

The Queen rose to full height from the ground, her white dress now heavy with the weight of the blood it had soaked up. She moved slowly, a macabre train trailing gore behind her. She kept her eyes locked on Cassandra's as she strode deliberately to where she stood. She placed her hands on Cassandra's hips and drew her close. Her hands snaked up Cassandra's waist, lightly over her breasts and up to her face. The metallic smell of the blood engulfed Cassandra as the Queen pulled her face closer with sticky red hands. Her eyes held a fevered shimmer. She licked Cassandra's lips and kissed her with an urgent hunger that expected a response.

Some time later Cassandra opened her eyes when she heard the crack of the door. She rolled over and poked her head up to see who was coming into the room. One of the maids tentatively peeked her head in to test the waters. Their eyes met and then came to rest on the lump of a dead man in a pool of black congealing blood. The girl's eyes widened and the door clicked shut again.

The Queen slept in the midst of the blood-streaked bed. Between the dried blood and the white feathers it looked as though several geese had also been sacrificed to sate the Queen's anger. She slept like a child, on her side peacefully curled and resting, feathers stuck here and there to her red-streaked brown skin. The plaited, jeweled wig was fully off now. Her curly hair damply stuck to her neck. She was naked but for the feathers and so was Cassandra.

Cassandra eased herself into a sitting position. Through the sheer curtains she could see the devastation. Bloody footprints, shards of earthenware, tables overturned, immeasurable treasure scattered on the golden marble floor, half hung curtains luffed in the afternoon breeze, the sea sparkled in the distance.

Cassandra herself was covered in bloody handprints. Her dress on the floor beyond the bed also marbled with red. She sighed and eased herself off the bed and onto her feet. She pulled her dress on and went to the door taking care not to step on any of the carnage or the gore. She opened the door just enough to let the maids in. If they were quiet the Queen would sleep for a while now. Cassandra put her fingers to her lips to make the point, but the shaking maids were far too frightened to engage in their normal chatter. They took in the scene from the edge of the room like lost children. One of them left and returned with linens, a broom and two eunuchs.

The enormous men took the linens from the girl and headed straight to the life-drained lump on the floor. Without ceremony they picked him up and dropped him onto a nearby carpet. The girls swept the rest of the debris off of the rug as they rolled him up and carried him out of the room on their shoulders after wiping their feet on more linens by the door before they left. The maids began to mop up the blood from the floor on their hands and knees. Soon they looked like walking corpses.

The Queen continued her nap.

Cassandra picked the book up from the floor and brought it over to the bed. None of the women dared go near them. Cassandra placed the book next to the sleeping Queen and tucked some of the ragged sheets around her so that she would not be so exposed. She pulled up a chair and waited. Someone brought in a table and set it with wine and fruit. She drank a cup down without taking a breath. She did not eat.

Cassandra changed into a gown one of the maids brought for her and sat back in the chair to continue her vigil. The form in the bed stirred and moaned.

"Cassandra?"

"I'm here, my Queen. I wait only on you." She said.

"Oh my lovely you brought the book to me, how sweet. You are always so thoughtful. I know you will help me."

"Of course, just tell me what you want me to do."

"I want you to stay here with me and decipher the book for me. I see only blank pages. That damned sorcerer must have put some kind of hex on it."

Cassandra did not think that was the case, but it was perilous to contradict the woman in the bed.

The Queen continued to talk through the curtains, "Come here love, I want you with me." Cassandra stood and unclasped

117

the gown, draped it over the chair and crawled back into the mess behind the curtains. Except for the chair and a few tables, the bed was the only remaining furniture in the room. Everything else had been removed.

Cassandra lay next to her lover and reached out to caress her hair like a mother soothing a disturbed child. After a bit the Queen sat up and pulled the book into her lap. She again tried to open it. "I need you my love."

Cassandra sat up and the Queen placed the book on her crossed legs. It opened easily to her touch; the text danced and sparkled on the page.

"What does it look like to you?"

"I see a golden radiant script in a language I do not know." As soon as Cassandra said this, the script seemed to morph again, she still did not recognize the lettering, but she understood the meaning almost as if the book itself communicated with her. "What does it look like to you?"

"I see only a blank page." She continued, "I have business to attend to. And I think Antony will arrive soon. I know this book is the key to my victory in the war against Octavian. You must not fail me. You will not leave this room. It is yours now. I will have everything you need brought to you. Learn this book. Figure out how to use the power within these pages. You are the only person I trust with it."

"For now..." thought Cassandra.

The Queen got off of the bed and snapped her fingers. The maids scurried out of their hiding places like frightened but obedient mice. The naked lady strode across the room as the others flowed behind in an uncertain wake. They disappeared through a door into a closet almost the size of the room they just left.

With shaking hands Cassandra opened the book again. The sparkling script breathed and shifted as though a breeze blew invisibly through the pages. The writing floated on the page as if it were not connected to it at all, as if the page and the words were in separate planes. She caressed it. The unknown golden words left the page and moved to her hand. Her entire hand glowed. Her skin sparkled and danced like waves in bright sunlight. She watched as the loving light moved up her arm. Heat and warmth expanded from her hand, through her arm and into her heart. A bubbly bliss spread through her being with each beat. Joyful tears flowed down her face. Exhaustion came from the back like a punch. She passed out on the bed.

When she woke up it was dark. Someone had lit a few of the torches on the walls and they gave a comfortable glow to the room. She put a hand down on the bed to rise and touched the book. She sat up and opened it again. The coded language in the breathtaking shimmering script was gone. She held her palm open in front of her face; her skin looked normal, but she felt a sense of calm and peace within her that had not existed before. It was not a dream.

She stood up and crossed the room to the mirror. Now she could see. Now she could really see. Her dark almond-shaped eyes had a new ring of fiery gold around the iris of brown. She stared at her new eyes - she did not remember Phisto having such eyes, nor any of the others.

"The book gives it's magic in a unique form to each person it chooses. And the book makes the choice, you cannot choose to receive the magic. Nor can you give it away. It is a specific gift."

"Who are you?" Cassandra asked the disembodied voice in her head. She had no fear. Spirits and other entities were not new to her.

"I am the ancient one of the book."

Morgan stopped to take a breath and looked at her watch. 2:30, almost time to go pick up the kids. The muses and the movie-story dissipated like clouds after a summer storm as her mind turned toward other things. She went upstairs and left the computer behind.

Day 24

"So I got some information on spirit guides."

Rachel's eyes widened as she forked the salad in front of her. "And?"

"Uhhh… well, I do have some, or at least one. I talked to her, or it. Because I have a thing about my thighs, I can hear her now."

"Her? Your thighs? What?"

"Well actually hear her, or it, again. She was my imaginary friend when I was a kid. Instead of being happier in a bathing suit, obsessively practicing hot yoga got me in shape to talk to spirit guides."

"That's not in the ads… but I still don't follow you."

"Somehow doing all that yoga did something to my head. She said it made my mind quieter and now I can talk to spirit guides."

Rachel laughed. "Maybe I have a new excuse to skip out. God knows the last thing I need is someone else bitching at me in my head."

"She seemed ok, she was laughing at me."

"Can you talk to her anytime?"

"I guess. I'm supposed to ask for help if I need it. I'm not sure they are up for chit-chat."

"So what did she tell you?"

"Not much other than what I told you so far. She can guide me, but she can't do *for* me. Like I'm on a treasure hunt and she's giving me clues."

"So she's not like a fairy godmother or something."

Morgan laughed, "No, I guess not. No pumpkin coaches for me."

"Can she help you find a new place to live? That'd be helpful."

"I don't know. I hadn't thought about that. I don't know if they do that sort of thing."

"I was kind of joking."

"Oh, sorry… that shows you where I am," said Morgan.

"Did you find a place yet?" asked Rachel.

"I can't think about it now. I might throw up." Morgan sat back and pushed her remaining salad away.

"So Ben is definitely losing the ex-pat package?" Rachel did not look directly at Morgan.

"Yes."

"All of it? They aren't going to pay for anything? Housing, schools, even the tax equalization?"

"Nope. Nothing. He'll be on a straight local salary if we stay here in London."

"Shit. That sucks. His salary isn't enough to keep you in the house and the kids at the same school?"

"Not even close… I mean rents are outrageous here in central London. I guess we're lucky they've paid for it this long."

"I'm so sorry." Rachel poked her fork around her salad without picking up anything.

"Ultimately these are princess problems. We'll have food on the table and a roof over our heads, but I've no idea where that roof will be right now."

"Can I do anything?" asked Rachel.

"Maybe I should just call Olivia."

Day 25

" Why don't you touch yourself?"

Morgan's eyes clicked open in the darkness. She teetered on the abyss of sleep when the voice spoke.

"Come on, you can feel me... touch yourself."

Ben snored next to her. There were no green whirling dervishes at the foot of the bed. This was not Ariadne or the Muses. She had only just met them, but she knew how they felt. Ariadne gave her a warm, hot tea feeling, the muses made it impossible for her not to smile; this presence had all the charm of a con artist. *"Shit, is this a demon?"* Morgan thought.

"Go ahead, snake that hand down between your legs. Let's see if you are wet." She felt a great weight on her head as though a giant bullfrog sat gloating over his prize catch. As much as it disturbed her, she was turned on. There was an undeniable buzzing between her legs, which felt different, but weirdly pleasant.

The 'bullfrog' reminded her of the taste of earwax.

"Come on... please. You know you want to. How long has it been? When was the last time your husband

125

touched you? Aren't you at all curious about what it would be like with me?"

"Who are you?"

"I'm a spirit."

"If you're a spirit, you can't have sex."

"How do you know what I can do? You feel me now, I know you do." The weight on her head began to merge with a sense of heaviness throughout her body. The presence managed to squeeze her... and then she began to feel him in other places.

"Come on, you have to help me here... I can do... a lot... but you have to touch yourself."

She was curious and turned on, as much as she hated to think about it, but she pushed back.

"No. I'm not interested. You can go."

This was greeted with silence. But the weight remained. She could sense frustration and stubborn resolve. Whoever, or whatever, this was, it wasn't done.

"Why are you here?"

"I'm here because you want me here."

"That's not much of an answer."

"I'm here to help you."

"Help me? What's your name?"

"Telemon."

"Telemon, what is it you want from me?"

126

"I want you to play..." Now there was a sense of laughter, as though she were the butt of an inside joke.

"I'm serious. I want you to leave."

Silence. The presence waited. She felt a growing sense of impatience and frustration.

"Do you have a message for me?"

Silence.

"Ariadne, please help me" thought Morgan.

"In what way?" asked Ariadne.

"I don't know, help me get rid of this thing."

"No, I can't do that."

Ben let out or rip-roaring snore and turned over.

"Ok, how can you guide me here? This spirit or whatever makes me very uncomfortable. I don't want it around."

"First you need to figure out why he is here."

"Why do I need to do that?"

"That may give you more information about what you need to do or learn."

"Can I just ignore him?"

Tinkling laughter filled her mind. *"Sure you could do that, but I doubt he is going to just go away now that he knows you can hear him. Once you are 'switched on' spirits will find you - you will be very attractive."*

"Are they all going to want sex?"

More laughter, *"I don't think so. They will come for different reasons... some may just need help getting to the light."*

"How would I know how to do that?"

"You will have all the help you need to do what is necessary at that time, there is nothing to worry about."

"A ghost wants to fuck me and you're telling me there's nothing to worry about? This is like something out of a horror movie."

Ariadne giggled, *"You will figure it out. You can do this."*

"But he's like a naughty school boy trying to see what he can get away with."

"And what is it that naughty schoolboys want?"

"Attention?"

"Why do they want attention?"

"Uhhhhhh... because they don't feel loved?"

"Exactly! They are looking for love."

"So what do I do?"

"When your kids are naughty, what do you do?"

"Depends on what they're doing. Sometimes I punish them."

"Does that work?"

"Most of the time, no... it's better if I talk to them and try to help them figure out why they did something, so they could make another choice next time."

"So you work with them in a loving and understanding way?"

"Yeah, I guess so."

"What works better, punishment or love?"

"Love."

"So there's your answer."

"But how do I show love to a spirit?"

"Open your heart. Tell him he is ok and that you want to help him, just like you would do with your kids."

"...That seems weird."

"Just see what happens. He came here for a reason - he may be able to help you as much as you can help him."

Morgan got up and went into the bathroom for a glass of water. When she crawled back into bed and pulled the covers up, Ben turned over again, still sound asleep. All the noise in her head felt like it was blasting through loud speakers, but it did not wake Ben.

"So... Telemon, what can I do for you?"

"I want to play with you."

"Why?"

"Because you are beautiful and I feel your body calling out to me."

"I don't feel my body calling out to you." That was a lie as Morgan was a little turned on, though she was still not sure why.

"Just the fact that I desire you, that is enough to turn you on. How long has it been since you felt desirable?"

Jeff was the first person to express a real interest in a long time. She and Ben had stopped having sex after Daisy was born.

"So you're here to show me I'm desirable?"

"I am here because I desire you."

"I appreciate that, but I don't want to fool around with you. It feels weird to me."

Morgan could sense a retraction in Telemon; the sensitive foot of a snail withdrawn. She felt him sulking.

"That doesn't mean I mind having you around. You can hang around if you want, I'm just not interested in getting physical."

She sensed a release in Telemon, but he did not speak. How she picked up on his feelings was a mystery.

She addressed Ariadne, *"Did I do ok?"*

"That was perfect! You were kind, but firm. You set the boundary with him, but did not reject him. He can hang around, but you will not be pressured to do things you are uncomfortable with. Well done."

"What now?"

"Maybe you go to sleep..."

Day 27

"I'm not going to church any more," declared Morgan.

"What do you mean? You're teaching catechism. You have to go to church. And Daisy's about to make her first communion." Ben barely looked at her as he spoke. It was a rare night when Ben was home for dinner. They had nearly finished a bottle of wine and the kids watched television in the next room.

"After Daisy makes her first communion and I finish my obligation with the catechism, I'm not going to church anymore," said Morgan.

"That's crazy talk. You have to go to church. You have to take the kids to church."

Morgan thought to herself, *"if you only fucking knew that we are all about to be struck dead. I'm fooling around with spirits and telepathy and god-knows-what-all. I shouldn't be anywhere near a fucking church."* But she said out loud, "I'm tired of dragging the kids to church. I'm not even sure I believe in any of it anymore. So if you want the kids to go, you can take them."

"What the fuck?"

Morgan repeated herself, "I'm tired of dragging the kids to church. I'm taking a break. If you want them to go, you can take them."

"Where's this going?" asked Ben.

"I don't know what you mean by that question. I never wanted to be a Catholic. I let you talk me into it. I'm done. If it's important to you that the kids go, no problem, you take them." Morgan got up and began to clear the dishes from dinner.

Ben drained the glass of red wine in front of him and left without offering to help. "I'm going out."

After Morgan attended to all the evening rituals alone, she found herself almost asleep in Daisy's bed. Sometimes Daisy still wanted Morgan to stay with her until she fell asleep at night. She pulled her arm out from under Daisy's pillow and tip-toed out of the room, closing the door behind her.

She peeked into Max's room next door. The light was on. He read one of his books.

"Which Horrible Histories book is that?"

"Cutthroat Celts." Said Max.

"Ahhhhh… charming."

"It's great. The Celts used to take the brains of those they defeated, cut the tops off their severed heads, mix the brains with clay and keep them as souvenirs. Isn't that awesome?"

"Again, charming… angel, it's time for you to go to bed. The blood-thirsty Celts will have to wait until tomorrow."

"Awwww Mom, c'mon, just a few more minutes, pleeeeease."

"How many pages until you finish that chapter?"

"Uhhh… two."

"Ok, read those."

Morgan sat on the edge of the bed while he finished the two remaining pages.

"Ok, now it's time for you to go to sleep."

"Mom, will stay with me for a few minutes?"

"Sure."

"Will you pet my hair?"

Morgan smiled, "Of course sweetie." Max faced the wall on his side as Morgan lay down to cuddle him. She stroked his hair and sang, 'Dona Nobis Pacem'. His shoulders relaxed as the day fell away. Morgan drifted.

"I like that song too."

Morgan looked at the sleeping child.

"But you are not my mother."

Morgan sat up and looked at Max.

"Not him. I guess you can't see me. He can see me." The soft weeping of a child crept into her mind.

Morgan sat up on the edge of the bed and peered into the darkness. All she could see was shelves of Horrible

Histories books and a collection of plastic dinosaurs. The moonlight poured in through the window making a windowpane cross on the carpeted floor. There was no one there she could see. *"Are you the little boy my daughter knows? The one in the pink knickers?"* asked Morgan in mind-speak.

"Yes."

"How long have you been here?"

"I don't know..." The voice trailed off into soft weeping.

"What's wrong?" asked Morgan.

"I need help..."

"What kind of help?"

"I've lost my mother."

"Lost your mother?"

"She used to live here, but something happened. I don't know. Now I can't find her but I'm scared to leave because I'm afraid that she'll come back and I'll miss her." More weeping.

"It's ok... How old are you?"

"Ten."

"Do you know how long you've been here?"

"No, but it seems like a long time."

The Kensington town house they currently occupied was nearly 200 years old. He could have been there for a very long time.

"Do you know what happened to you?"

"No, I was sick and my mother cried a lot. And then she couldn't hear me anymore and then one day she left. I haven't seen her since."

"Ok. I hate to ask this question but...is it possible that you died?"

The weeping Morgan could hear grew stronger.

"I-I-I dooooooon't knooooow."

"It's ok sweetie, it's ok. I think you died and that's why your mother couldn't hear you anymore. I think she left because she had no idea you were still here."

"Buuuut where is sheeeeeee?" The weeping turned to wailing.

"Shhhhhhh...Honey it's ok. I think I can help you."

"You do?" Morgan sensed as much as heard the hiccupping associated with stifled sobs.

"Yes. I think you've been here a long time and I think it's long enough that your mother has died too," soft moans echoed in her head, *"I think she's looking for you in the afterlife. I can help you find her."*

"Can you?"

"What's your favorite story?"

"Aladdin and the Den of Thieves."

"Oh, that's a great story. I love that one too, especially the part about the flying carpet. Do you remember the part about the flying carpet?"

"I love the flying carpet. He can go anywhere!"

Things played out in Morgan's head almost as fast as she spoke. The idea barely formed and came out without thought. She felt like a stereo system for the netherworld.

"You can go anywhere too. Let's call that flying carpet for you." In her inner vision, she saw the carpet waiting in the air as a little boy in pink knickers pulled himself up onto it. A light as bright as the sun shone in the sky somewhere other than the room where she sat on the edge of Max's bed. *"Now I want you to think of your mother and call to her. She's in the light and she will be there waiting for you. Just tell the magic carpet to take you toward the light."* The little boy turned around and waved at Morgan as the carpet took him toward the light. She watched until he and the carpet disappeared into the light.

She sat on the edge of Max's bed for a few minutes. Silence rested around her like a comfortable blanket until she became aware of Max's slow sleep breaths next to her. The window of moonlight on the floor had shifted. She stared at it dazed. She felt heavy. She almost rolled into Max's bed next to him but thought better of it. She touched the top of his head and pulled the door closed behind her. She found her way to her own bed where she collapsed next to the computer.

The Muses bounced into view.

"You did it, you did it! You saved the little boy!"

"I didn't exactly save him, I showed him where to go. But how did I know what to do?"

"You can do anythinngggggggg. This. Is. Easy. For. You!" The muses did a bizarre pole dance using the posts on her bed. They flung themselves from one to the other as they spoke.

"I just knew what to say, but I don't know how. Did you help me?"

"We. Are. Always. Helping. Yoooouuuuuuu."

"Well thank you! That was… it was… pretty fucking cool. Did we really do that?"

"Yes, you did! You are welcommmmmmmmmmme… We love youuuuuuuuuuu." And as quickly as they had come, they were gone.

Or not quite gone. A lone muse popped his (her?) head up from the end of the bed; *"Now write about it!"* then disappeared again. Morgan did.

Day 30

"Morgan, you're really skinny. Are you eating?" Rachel pulled a sweater over her damp head as they attempted to get dried off and dressed in the bump and grind of a too small dressing room with twenty-five other sweaty ladies.

"I haven't really been very hungry." Morgan found a piece of bench to perch on while threading her wet legs into leggings.

Rachel leaned in closer to Morgan. "Is there more going on?"

"Yeah. Lots of weird stuff."

"I think it's time for another drink."

"I'll pass out if I drink something now."

"Fine, we'll go for coffee. I'll meet you outside." Rachel shouldered her bag and fled the dressing room.

Once Morgan pulled free of the mess in the changing room they walked to a coffee shop near the tube stop at Parson's Green.

They settled into a booth with steaming, oversized, white cups in front of them. "Catch me up," said Rachel as she blew on the foam heart floating on top of her coffee.

Morgan sighed. "So I talked to my spirit guide, talked to some ghosts and got introduced to three weird little creatures who call themselves muses who are supposed to help me write and maybe see past lives or something. Just saying it out loud to you makes it sound even crazier than I already feel."

"Shit. No wonder you look like crap. You've been talking to spirits? Like a medium? What are they telling you?"

"I don't know. Things like, I have to ask for their help and I need to be practicing communicating with them…Oh and that I can help send spirits to the light." She did not mention Telemon.

"Holy crap. Are you serious? Is it scary?"

"Not most of the time, just weird. They are like voices in my head, like the telepathy but no one's there. And apparently Daisy can see ghosts too, and talk to them."

"Daisy?"

"Yeah, I forgot to tell you about that. We were playing cards and I kept hearing this voice and then I knew she could hear it too because she was using the ghost to cheat."

"What? Stop a minute. Daisy was talking to a ghost and cheating at cards and you could both hear the voice?"

"Yeah. Only she didn't know I could hear it too. She didn't tell me because she thought I might be scared."

Now Rachel laughed, "Oh God Morgan, this is way beyond me. What do you do now?"

"Ride it out? Ask for help from my spirit guides? Drink? I've noticed I can't really tune in as well when I'm drinking. I just keep thinking, 'shit, what's next?' And then I still have to figure out what the hell to do about finding a new place to live. And I have no idea how much money we have to work with, Ben is being really cagey about it all." Morgan stirred the coffee in front of her.

"I wish I knew how to help you honey."

"You're helping me just by sitting there, talking to me, and not suggesting I go see a psychiatrist."

"I know, but I wish there was more I could do. I have no idea how you are managing to stay upright and do anything, I'd be on drugs by now."

"It's like there are two of me or something. One part of me feels like this is natural, like it's more real than anything else. It feels kind of...right. And then the intellectual side of me is screaming, 'ARE YOU CRAZY?'. In a way, I'm much more stressed out about the financial situation. I mean, am I going to have to move back to New Orleans with Daisy? Move in with my parents?"

"It'll all work out, it'll be ok." Rachel reached out to touch Morgan's forearm resting on the table. She squeezed her and continued, "Are you taking the kids away for spring break?"

"I'm just taking them to my parents' house in North Carolina. It'll feel like a vacation, but will only cost the plane tickets which at least this time the company is still paying for. Where are you going?"

"Nowhere at the moment. The kids' schools are off on different weeks, so it looks like I'm stuck here for now. Want me to look at some places with Olivia?"

"It's ok, thanks. Ben is supposed to get a budget together for real so I can work with her as soon as I get back."

Morgan settled into her airplane seat. *"This is the last time in business class,"* she thought, *"No more expat package means no more fancy plane tickets."*

The muses did not seem to mind. They dressed their round green bodies in steward jackets and pretended to serve drinks to the unseeing passengers as the final few people paraded down the aisle before the cabin door closed.

"Guys, what are you doing?"

"We're having fffuuuuuuuuuuuuun." As soon as they spoke they started to move. Now they jumped up on springy legs to hit the ceiling of the cabin and then pingponged between the ceiling and the floor. Morgan tried not to laugh or look at them as they landed in passengers' laps and gave elaborate apologies in British accents. .

"Oh 'scuuuuuse me darling...I didn't mean to muss your hair... are you sure that shade of lipstick is the right choice? I don't knoooooooooooow."

"Can I take your jacket?" asked a flight attendant.

"Yes, thank you." said Morgan as she handed the jacket to the smiling, suited woman.

"Yes thank you. Yes thank you. Yes thaaaaaaank you!" repeated the muses in turn.

"Ok guys, time to go underground." The muses gave her puppy dog eyes and dutifully disappeared.

"Mom are you talking to me? How can I go underground?" asked Max.

"Oh, right, yes, sorry. I was just, I was just, just uhhhhh...thinking out loud. Never mind. Are you ok? You got a book and your iPad? Headphones?"

"Yup. Got it all and my seatbelt. See?"

"Great. Good job."

"It's not like it's my first time Mom." Max tipped his iPad and returned to his game.

Morgan turned to Daisy. "You ok angel?"

"Yes Mommy, I love you. Hold my hand please." Daisy reached over the seat to take Morgan's hand.

"Baby we haven't even pushed back from the gate. Are you scared?"

"No, I just want to hold your hand."

"Ok." Morgan squeezed the little girl's hand. Morgan was loath to leave London with so much uncertainty, but Ben had convinced her to go. He had promised to finish putting together a budget while they were gone. She was going to cut their spring break short by a week so she could return early, but a week in the mountains of North

143

Carolina at her parents' home was a welcome respite from the chaos her London life had become.

Day 38

North Carolina

Morgan's mother picked them up at the airport in Atlanta and drove them the two and half hours to the mountain house outside of Cashiers. Morgan felt herself exhale as they turned up the steep, grey, gravel driveway observed by the hemlocks and pine trees to the house of her mother's heart. The kids tumbled out of the car and raced inside to argue over who got to sleep in the top bunk.

"So, how are you really?" asked her mother, without moving to get out of the car.

"Exhausted."

"What's going on with Ben?"

"I have no idea. He promised to give me a real budget when we get back so I can try to find a place for us to live. Who knows? I may end up back in New Orleans."

"Do you mean you might get a divorce?"

"I think anything could happen. I've no idea." Morgan got out of the car to end the conversation. Morgan's mother collected herself and followed her into the house, allowing the screen door to slap behind her.

Morgan stood in the middle of the large front porch and listened to the sound of a nearby wet weather stream. The blonde wood, vaulted ceiling rose at least 20 feet above her head. A stacked stone fireplace stood quietly behind her. It was her favourite spot. She inhaled the pine and a faint scent of smoke from a fire recently burnt. In the distance she could see dark clouds formed a front just beyond the reach of the mountains. Morgan hoped for the beauty of a booming thunderstorm to watch from a cushy chair on the screened-in porch.

That evening, after the kids and Morgan's parents had gone to bed, Morgan had a front row seat as the wished-for thunderstorm played out all around her. A fresh flash of lightning illuminated her surroundings and revealed a man dripping with rain outside the screen door. Startled, she sat up and wondered if the screen was latched and if she could grab a fire iron before he got to her.

"Please help me." He said.

"What?" Morgan realized that he communicated in mind-speak. Was he a spirit? She could see him and that confused her.

"Can I come out of the rain?" he asked.

"Of course." Morgan's heart raced; surely this was a spirit. He continued to stand outside despite her invitation. He pulled at the door handle, but the door did not move.

"Why can't I open the door?"

"I don't know. Where did you come from?" The hair on the back of Morgan's neck rose, but she stood and moved toward the door.

"I'm sorry to bother you, I...I was up on the trail hiking and something happened. I can't seem to get out of here. I can't seem to get anyone to hear me."

Morgan opened the screen door. He stepped in dripping wet, but the floor under him was dry. She was right, he was not in her realm. The whole scene played out in her mind. He had a heart attack on the trail. He died without warning, no idea he was sick. He was unprepared. Now the confused spirit waited for response. *"How long have you been on the trail?"*

"I don't know. It's all so weird. It was Friday when I started hiking. But I seem to be stuck here now."

It was Monday evening. He must have died on Friday. His spirit had wandered the woods for three days. *"I hate to ask this, but is it possible that you died on the trail?"*

"What? What are you talking about? Oh shit... maybe... I was on the trail alone, hiking up to Chimneytop... and then I was in the forest and it was raining. There were people all around. I could see myself lying on the ground, but no one could hear me. Was that ambulance there for me?"

147

"I think so… I don't know. I think something must have happened to you up there. I'm so sorry."

"How come you can hear me?"

"I can hear spirits. And I guess I can see them now too. I think I can help you." Morgan sensed that this was true but she had no idea how. He probably wouldn't go for a flying carpet.

"How?" he asked.

"I think you died so suddenly and unexpectedly that you got lost instead of going to the light. I can help you get there." The words just occurred to her and she followed their lead.

"Okay…" he was confused and not yet convinced.

"What's your favorite song?" Morgan asked.

"What the hell does that have to do with anything?"

"I know it seems weird, but go with it."

"Help Me Make It Through The Night, the Kris Kristofferson version."

Morgan could not help but smile. "Play it in your mind." Even as she told him to do this, the song began to play for both of them.

"Dance with me?" she asked.

"I don't think my wife would like that very much."

Again Morgan smiled. *"Oh, of course, I understand."*

"This song actually makes me think of my horse."

"Where is your horse now?" asked Morgan.

"She died a long time ago."

"Call her." The thought and her words occurred simultaneously.

A beautiful chestnut mare stood in the gravel driveway.

"How did you do that?" he asked.

"I didn't. You did. Go ride her. She will take you where you need to go."

Morgan had no idea how she knew this, but she did. Without another word the man turned and went through the opened door. He climbed into the waiting saddle and the horse lifted itself off the ground. Morgan watched her go as a crack of light opened the sky and the spirit on the flying horse disappeared.

Day 39

The next morning Morgan sat at the breakfast table with her family.

"Morgan, did you see the article in The Crossroads Chronicle about that poor man?" asked her mother.

"What poor man?" asked Morgan.

"That poor man who died on the trail up to Chimneytop. He was from Alabama."

"What are you talking about Mom?"

"Last Friday before you got here. I can't believe I forgot to mention it. He went on a solo hike and had a heart attack or something on the trail. Some hikers from the High Hampton found him and called the paramedics. You should've heard the ruckus - all the sirens came up our road here. They had to hike in and bring him out."

"Holy shit. That was real." thought Morgan.

Day 40

"Mom, are you on the phone again? I thought we were going out in the boat."

"Yeah, sorry. Ok. Two secs. Get your shoes on."

Morgan put the phone on the table and looked out toward the lake. The steep hill dropped away from the cabin at a shocking angle and disappeared under the pines until it met the shining water, spread out like quixotic mercury. There were dark clouds in the distance but they moved away.

"Come on Mom." Max was impatient.

"What's up? Did your iPad break?" asked Morgan.

"It's out of battery. I can't find my charger."

"So he took mine," said Daisy.

"I asked."

"No, you didn't!"

"Ok, ok, let's just go. Where are your shoes?" asked Morgan.

"Why do we need shoes for the boat?"

"You need shoes to walk down the hill to the boat."

"No we don't." responded Max. Daisy looked sideways at her brother.

"Whatever. I'm not going to fight with you about it. Let's just go," said Morgan.

Someone had pressed log pieces into the hillside like steps in an attempt to make the descent less treacherous. They had not succeeded. The slimy moss that now grew over the rotten wood ensured that getting down the hill to the water still took skill. Morgan preferred shoes. The muses threw themselves headlong down the hill rolling and tumbling until they arrived bouncing and breathless by the edge of the water.

"WHHEEEEEEEEEEE!".

Their flat-bottomed, aluminum skimmer rocked in the wake of a ski boat that passed. It bumped and jostled sideways and up and down at the same time. A small outboard motor attached to the back. A red canoe rested upside down on the weathered dock acting as a convenient cave for spiders.

"Max, you hold the side while Daisy gets in please."

He squatted down and pulled the green metal up against the dock.

"Can you take any longer?" asked Max. Daisy loitered to get at him for pinching the charger.

"I don't want to fall in." Said Daisy.

The muses made squinty eyes at Max and then went to balance on top of Daisy's head, all three stacked up on top of one another making for a flimsy green tower that shifted in an exaggerated way every time she moved.

Morgan cringed but kept her mouth shut and held the boat for Max as he dropped all his weight into the back. The boat kicked up and knocked her backwards onto the dock.

"Oh shit. Sorry Mom." The muses bounced out of the boat as if they could assist Morgan to her feet.

"Don't say that, it's a bad word. You owe me another dollar," said Daisy.

Morgan shot her son a look as he glared at the back of his sister's smiling head. She picked herself up and held the dock with one hand while she stepped down shifting her bum onto the seat in the middle.

Max pulled the cord and the engine sputtered awake. She pushed off from the dock as the boat turned toward the middle of Lake Glenville.

"Where are we going?" Asked Daisy.

"Yes. Where are we going? Where are we going?" Morgan tried to ignore the mind-speak of the muses and focus on her kids and the boat.

"I wanna go check out that cove we passed the other day. It looked like there might be a cave there," said Max.

"Ok," replied Daisy.

Daisy turned around to look at her mother and held out her hand. It was an awkward angle. Morgan leaned forward with her arm stretched out. Wind, not the speed of the boat, lifted her hair and then played with it, trying to stick it in her mouth. The clouds in the distance were darker.

Max revved the engine and the bow lifted a bit. Daisy's weight was not enough to hold anything down. She faced forward on the seat with her arm twisted behind her so she could continue to hold Morgan's hand.

The clouds had changed direction. The wind picked up and the scent of rain pressed itself upon them.

"Hey Max, maybe we should turn back. I thought that storm was going the other way."

Max was not to be daunted. "No, I think we're ok. It'll probably just be a little shower or something. I told you we shouldn't have waited so long."

Morgan took a deep breath and practiced her patience. No response was the best response. The wind worked harder to give her a new hairstyle.

"I should have put on a hat," thought Morgan. The muses now sat in her lap with hats on and giggled. *"You guys don't have any hair,"* she thought.

"We do too! Look." And with that they took off their hats revealing cascades of curly golden hair.

Morgan smiled and stifled a laugh.

The lake began to pick up a chop which Morgan did not like. "Max, I'm sorry but this isn't looking good. I really think we need to turn back." As she said this she realized that she had forgotten the life jackets on the dock.

"Mom you worry too much." He glared ahead at the horizon.

"Max. I'm telling you to turn around now." The sky broke open with a crack as lightning streaked its way down to the water so close they felt the buzz of electricity and smelled the charge. Daisy screamed out and fell backwards. At first Morgan thought she might have been hit. She huddled in the bottom of the boat scared but unscathed.

"Shit. That was close." Max jerked the handle on the motor back toward himself in an attempt to turn the skiff back to the dock. A wave hit the side of the boat and they rocked sideways almost tipping over. The motor sputtered and died on the spot.

"What the fuck." Max recovered and tried in vain to twist the handle and get the motor to turn on again. Without any speed to counteract the increased wave action, the boat began to rock and jump at the command of wind and water. There were no oars in the boat.

"Mom, what do we do?" The rain came down, drenching them. The temperature dropped at least ten degrees in the rocking, tipping boat. Another crack of thunder plunged a bolt of lightning into the water only a little farther away from the reeling boat. Swimming was not an option. Max could probably make it, but not Daisy.

Even the muses were huddled under the seat in front of Morgan. *"You can fix this. You can make this go away."*

"What are you talking about?" Thought Morgan.

"You can stop this storm. You can make it ok. Don't you know that?" asked the muses.

"How would I ever do that?"

"Well we don't know how. We just know you can."

"That's helpful. Thanks. We are all gonna die out here and I could have done something, but you don't know what and I don't know what."

"Think about it and trust yourself. Pleeeasssse."

Morgan thought of Ariadne and was told, *"The name of the wind is Chaos."*

"Mom, what do we do?"

"Just keep trying to get the motor going. Slow down. Take a breath. We're still in the boat. Just keep trying. You can do it."

Morgan inhaled deeply as the wind continued to whip her now wet hair into her mouth, it stung her eyes, everywhere at once.

"Chaos the wind... can you help me? Can you show me what to do?" Morgan exhaled and as she did a tornado formed in her mind, the small vortex of which sprang from the crown of her head and rose with increasing size toward the black sky. She imagined spreading the

156

top of the cyclone wide overhead so that it blocked the cloud above like a protective umbrella. The rain stopped falling on them. Morgan closed her eyes and inhaled until her chest expanded like a balloon then exhaled and imagined her breath blowing the clouds away to the East. The waves slowed down, the boat eased it's frantic rocking.

"Mom I think the rain stopped." Max turned to the motor and worked with the choke to get it started again.

"Baby are you ok?" Daisy sprang into Morgan's lap from the bottom of the boat in response.

"Shit Daisy. Don't do that. You almost knocked us over again." Said Max.

They both ignored him and Morgan hugged the little girl under her shoulder. She felt the wind stir and rain began to fall again. The tornado umbrella faded. The muses jumped with enthusiasm on the seat Daisy abandoned earlier.

"You have to keep doing it. Keep doing it! Concentrate or we all die!" They giggled and bounced. *"Oh except for us. We don't die!"* All three muses leapt from the boat into the water and disappeared.

As soon as Morgan remembered the cyclone and stuck it back on her head like an enormous upside down party hat, the rain stopped. Now she imagined clawing back the clouds with gargantuan hands to reveal the blue sky hidden above. The clouds parted and the storm above the cyclone dissipated, evaporating like smoke on a windy day.

The motor started with a pop and the boat shot forward. "Sorry about that. Where are we going now?"

"Home." Said Morgan. "I'm not at all sure about this crazy weather".

"It's all over with now."

"I know but let's go tomorrow after everything is clear." Morgan was not confident she would be able to maintain the bizarre protection or if she could end the storm. Maybe she had just created space for them to get back. She was not even sure how she did it.

"All that matters is that it's working." The muses peeked at her over the side of the boat as they hung onto the edge.

Max scowled at Morgan, but turned the boat back toward the dock.

"I don't ever want to go out on the lake again." said Daisy.

"Oh sweetie, that was just a freak storm. We're fine. It'll be fun to go tomorrow." She gave Daisy a reassuring jostling hug, but Daisy did not look convinced.

They pulled back into the dock, tied the boat off and clambered back up the treacherous steps to the house. The muses enjoyed slipping and sliding on the moss covered hill, so she left them to it.

As she closed the door to the house behind them she thought, "*Well now it can rain.*" Thunder clapped overhead and a deluge dropped all at once like God had turned a too-full bucket over. Out of nowhere it poured.

The muses meekly stepped in as Morgan shooed the wet children out of the room to change their clothes. Water formed puddles around the three green creatures as they stood near the door. Morgan did not bother to scold them as the water was contained in whatever realm they made their existence, so no mess on her floor. Morgan was chilled and wet to her underwear, but she questioned the Muses.

"*Ok. Now you guys have to explain what just happened.*" thought Morgan.

"*What? That? It was nothing for you.*"

"*It hardly seems real to call you guys nuts. But you are nuts. Down to your little green toes, if you have toes. Or I'm nuts. I've no idea anymore. Can you please just explain that?*" asked Morgan.

"*You calmed the sea and you stopped the storm. You're Jesus!*"

"*I'm not fucking Jesus. Ugh. AHHHHHHH. Really? What the hell? What did I just do? Did I do that or not?*"

Now the muses were balanced on top of each other and using the coffee table as a platform. Morgan could hear the sound of shots being fired from the Xbox in the room below. A vague smoke smell pervaded the room, a hangover from a fire in the fireplace the night before. The smell of dinner cooking should have been in the air.

"We don't know what happened. We are just your muses. We didn't do it, but we knew you could. All you had to do was ask for help. You can do lots of stuff, you just don't believe you can."

Then they popped like bubbles and disappeared. Morgan was too agitated to be creative.

"Ariadne can you help explain this please?" asked Morgan as she made her way to her room. She had to get some dry clothes.

"You have powers you do not understand, that you have not tapped into in this lifetime. Powers you have always had."

"You've said that, but this is all a surprise to me. How did I just do that?"

"You asked for help and you got it."

"But why did I get the help? Why would I get help and not someone else? Why can't just anybody do this?"

"There are many reasons, but the main one is you have to be friends with these forces. And then there is another important factor too."

"I'm not friends with Chaos the wind."

"You have been very close to Chaos at other times and even if you don't remember that, Chaos does," said Ariadne.

"Ok, I've no idea what to think of that. Does Chaos talk?"

"No. Chaos is a force, an ancient force that no longer needs to speak. It just is."

"What's the other factor?"

"Chaos will not respond if he feels his force is being misused. He has to trust you. Controlling the weather is not a magic trick to be shown off to your friends. One must have reverence for these primal forces."

"So you're telling me that the wind trusts me? The wind. The thing that makes tornadoes and hurricanes trusts me?" asked Morgan.

"Yes!"

"Because we have a prior association?"

"Yes."

"The wind trusts me?"

"Yes. But not just Chaos…"

"I can't talk about this anymore."

"In truth, you are a friend to all of the elementals." said Ariadne.

"All of the elementals? Wait. Does that include the fire?"

"Yes, exactly. Wind, fire…"

"Mom, I'm hungry." Morgan found herself back in the den with Daisy at the top of the basement stairs. "Mom, are you ok?"

"Yeah. Sorry honey, I'm just tired. What do you want for dinner?"

"Can we have spaghetti?" Daisy asked as Morgan looked at her with an arched eyebrow and a half smile. "Please" finished the child.

Morgan reached out to pull Daisy closer. She responded by dropping on to the couch and engaging in a momentary cuddle. She released herself and said, "Thanks Mom," as she disappeared down the stairs.

"Shall we continue?" Inquired Ariadne.

"What with the crazy stuff like I'm friends with all the elemental forces of the earth?"

"Ahhhh, yes. You can remember anytime you like. Just start writing."

"Ok."

"Just ask the question and let it flow."

"I have to make dinner first."

"Do it whenever you want. The more you practice any of these skills the easier it will get. You are not learning new skills, only remembering what you already know."

Max wandered upstairs drawn by the call of his stomach. Morgan turned off the spirit channel to make dinner. She pulled out pasta and set the water to boil. Heating a pan with some oil she fried off ground meat that needed to be eaten. It sizzled as it hit the pan, filling the kitchen with the hunger-inducing smell of searing meat. She opened a jar of tomato sauce and heated that too.

Max watched Morgan bustle around the kitchen. "Angel, you could lend me a hand."

"I sure hope that pasta's not for me. You do recall that I hate pasta?" said Max.

Morgan rescued some burger from the pan to make a patty as if that had been her plan all along. "Max please look in the cabinet for a bun."

Max pulled a bag of buns out and put them on the counter. Then he grabbed a bottle of sparkling water and headed downstairs.

"Life would be easier if you liked pasta." she called after him.

"Sorry…" echoed up from the basement.

After the three of them ate, Morgan asked the kids to clean up the plates and the kitchen.

"Mom, really? Where are Pappy and Nana?" asked Daisy.

"They went out with some friends tonight. Look, I've some work to do on the computer and it'd be helpful to me. Thank you very much for being such loving children." Daisy rolled her eyes, gathered a plate and utensils from the table and took them to the sink. Max got up and followed her with his plate.

Morgan picked up her computer, sat on the couch and thought, *"Ok, guys...just for fun, show me how I know the wind."*

The muses popped out of the chimney flue with a flourish. *"At. Your. Service."*

The image of the Egyptian room returned to her inner vision. Morgan typed.

"So what is it that you would have me do, Ancient One of the Book?" asked Cassandra.

"I would have you learn. I will reintroduce you to the forces of nature. Accept that you are one with them, indivisible. We do not have much time. But we will make the most of it."

The room burst into flames. She looked for a way out, but flames surrounded the bed. The hangings on the bed were alight. As her eyes searched for escape, she noticed she felt no heat from the flames, nor was there any smoke. From the center of the flames a woman as black as an inky, starless night appeared, her eyes bright coals pressed into tarry darkness.

"I am Samantha, keeper of the flame." Samantha held her hand out to Cassandra, her naked torso glistening in the light. *"Come, let the flames purify you. There is nothing to be afraid of, only the purest of bodies will be able to withstand the work you must do."*

Cassandra took the hand offered and stood next to the dark figure. Flames caught the white gown she wore. She was consumed by fire. She smelled nothing but the incense burning and felt only a slight tickle all over her body. No searing heat, no burning flesh, no smell of singed hair. When Samantha was satisfied Cassandra was pure, she released her to the bed. Cassandra looked up again, and the room was dark, untouched, as if she had only awoken from a dream.

Next Cassandra found herself in a boat floating in blackness. It was impossible to discern night sky from water until glowing shapes flitted and twirled just beneath the surface. Unearthly voices burst from the depths. A moon appeared, casting glitter on the surging waves of the sea. The water fairy light swirled and danced around and around the craft, moving faster and faster as the voices reached a crescendo. Cassandra understood the language of the Naiads.

"We are the maids of the water swimming wild and free. We are the maids of the water-" The chorus rose out of the deep like so many tinkling bells. And then, one bubbling voice cut through the others like laughter. *"Cassandra, please join us."*

Cassandra sat back, *"I thank you for your kind offer, but I think there are things I must do first."*

The ringing crystal voice replied, *"You are always welcome. If you ever need help up here please do not hesitate to ask. We are at your service until you return to us."*

The lights and the singing ended like a snuffed candle. Cassandra was cloaked in sudden darkness and utter silence.

She found herself in the desert. The sun shone on the sands all around her, nothing but a vast expanse of undulating earth. The ground beneath her shook and the sands shifted. Cassandra was there, but felt neither the heat, nor was moved by the shifting of the ground. A ghost on the scene, witness to everything and subject to nothing.

A face appeared on the sand as if a giant statue lay just beneath the dune and pressed it's features skyward but not quite enough for the ground to uncover the figure beneath. The face of the Earth opened her mouth and swallowed all that was around it. Her eyes blinked open, lit by the molten core of the planet. She spoke; *"Cassandra, I know you. We played together before I was born, and we shall be together again. You can count on me for anything you might need. I shall be summoned by the very thought of me. All that I have, I offer you."*

"Why should I be so graced?"

"Because you are one of us. The one in whom all the elements meet. In this and many lifetimes to come."

"I don't understand."

"You are the great balancer. The one who walks the path between creation and destruction, light and dark. You have been, and will be, called many names: Ma'at, Morrigan, Lila, Adrestia, Nemesis, Mary, Woman. You are a part of us, all the Elementals, as much as we are a part of you and all the human race. You are at once Elemental and Divine." The face sank below the surface and disappeared. Cassandra found herself back in her room. The now empty book sat on the table next to her.

A gust from the river caught the curtains like sails billowing in full bloom. A coolness pervaded the air, perfumed with the scent of jasmine. The air blew harder pushing the curtains away from the window. Something stopped her from going to close the shutters. Fingers of breeze caressed her face and played with her hair. Her gown fluttered and rose with the draft, dropping again to eddy near her feet. The smell of rain came in with the wind; the metallic snap and freshness of a cool shower without the water.

A sensuous voice filled her mind, echoing; *"My adored, I am so glad to have you back with me again. I have missed you so. Could you not feel me? I am as always at your command. There is nothing I will not do for you."*

"And you are?"

"I am Chaos the wind, known, like you, by many names: the agent of change, I am quickening in the womb, I am the ubiquitous destroyer. Twins, you and I have been lovers since the beginning of time. At once passionate and teasing and hateful - how I have ached for you."

Cassandra heard thunder stalking in the distance and felt the resonance in her chest as if she were part of it too. One last caress from the unseen Chaos and everything went still.

The Queen slipped into bed with her. Cassandra had gotten used to these sudden appearances in and out of bed.

The Queen ran her fingers down the curve of Cassandra's hips. "What are we learning, my lovely? Things are moving quickly. I'll need your help very soon. Today I want you with me when I meet the generals. You should know what the plans are so that you can see where we might be able to intervene."

"As you wish."

"So tell me, what have you learned? What new sorcery can you teach me?"

Cassandra sighed, "There is nothing I can teach you. The magic of this book is not incantations, it is more an understanding of the existing magic of the world. It is not something that can be taught. It simply is."

The Queen's nails dug into Cassandra's waist, "You know what happens to traitors who defy me?"

"My Queen, I know you are not to be crossed. But neither can I lie to you. If you do not believe me, there is nothing I can do. The book has given itself to me, not because I chose it, but because it chose me. Something I'm only beginning to understand." Cassandra looked directly at the Queen as she spoke.

"I have always trusted you, but greed and lust for power can turn anyone into a traitor. I did not imagine that would happen to you. I thought you loved me." Cleopatra stretched across the pillow to kiss Cassandra as she began to explore her body with her hands. Cassandra tried to relax and give in, but she knew the endgame.

Her lover stiffened and turned onto her back. "Octavian is on the way with two-hundred ships. Even if you do not love me, surely you would not like to see this place as an outpost of Rome?"

"What will be, will be."

"And how true that will be, my dear love." The Queen rolled out of bed and stood in one swift motion. She snapped her fingers as the guards poured into the room. Cassandra did not resist as she was pulled naked from the bed and escorted out of the room.

It was early morning, so only the servants were up and about in the palace.

Cassandra walked head held high in the center of a phalanx of guards. So many guards for a small, naked woman, the Queen must have feared what she was capable of.

The bristling group of guards left the palace with their charge and walked through the nearly empty city. As the sun rose, the inhabitants would begin to show themselves when they left their homes for the morning markets that were waking up all over town.

At the city gates they loaded Cassandra into a cage-like wagon drawn by donkeys. Again they surrounded her as though an army were in danger of coming to rescue her. She could feel the sun rising into the sky to witness the journey. The wind caressed her. The power of the desert earth sang to her. Chaos offered to blow them away, Gaia offered to swallow them and Samantha would have taken special pleasure in creating a conflagration. Cassandra refused.

"It is not yet time," she told them in her mind.*"Very soon I will ask your*

help, but this has to be the way it is for now. Soon I will join you all. I have a few more things to do. Thank you. I am grateful for your offers of help."

At the port Cassandra was transferred to one of the Queen's ships. The slaves below rowed downriver to Luxor. Another cart took the company to a high desert wall near the tomb of Hatshepsut and Cassandra's final home carved into the outcropping. A cave yawned in front of her. A large rock rested nearby.

The cage was opened and Cassandra stepped down. She walked unbidden into the cave. It was not deep, high or set. A simple dry place that appeared to have been purpose carved. The men set to work rolling the rock in front of the entrance in order to seal it.

She sat naked in the dirt and thought about how long she might have left. She took a deep breath in the darkness and lay flat on the ground. She had to wait.

Some time later she awoke and sat up. A presence was near. Samantha's crackling voice reverberated in the cave. *"Would you like some light?"*

"That and some heat," replied Cassandra.

"Then make it." The crackling turned to laughter.

"I... I don't know how."

"Don't you realize we are all a part of you now? You embody each of the elementals. You are our child and each of us resides within you," said Samantha.

"I don't know what that means." Whispered Cassandra.

"You are so much more powerful than you know. You could leave this place if you wanted to."

"I feel it is not my time to do that. If you help me, I can accomplish what I need to from here."

"You are quite right. We will do it together. But until then you might as well make yourself comfortable. Make yourself some fire."

"How?"

"Put out your hand and think 'fire'," said Samantha.

Cassandra put her hand out into the darkness. She could feel it, but not see it. The image of flame came into her mind and a ball of fire appeared, causing her hand to emerge from the darkness.

"But I have no wood."

"Gaia has left you a present, look," said Samantha.

Cassandra moved her hand holding the cold flame toward Samantha's voice. A pile of wood sat on the floor of the cave.

"Now throw it," commanded Samantha.

Cassandra tossed the unburning ball of fire into the circle. It burst into flame, except now warmth came from it too.

Samantha spoke again, *"If you were to stick your hand into it, it would not burn you, though it gives light and warmth. It will not smoke or consume the wood. It will be here as long as you are."*

She was at peace. She lay back against the wall and realized that she had down cushions surrounding her. She relaxed into them and closed her eyes.

A panorama of scenes played on her closed lids, as if she had a pair of binoculars trained in the distance and could look anywhere her mind gave her interest to see. The first scenes came unbidden. She saw Cleopatra arguing with Antony and then pleading with him as he left in full battle gear. She saw hundreds of ships on the horizon. She saw the flags.

She switched her focus to her mother and brothers. She had not seen them for so long. Tears came to her eyes and washed down her cheeks as she watched her mother kneading bread while the youngest of her brothers played at her feet in a squat. She had only seen him as a baby and not since. She imagined hugging her mother from behind as she worked, clutching her around the waist and pressing her cheek into her warm back, the scent of yeast surrounding them both. She felt her mother's hand reach back to squeeze her arm and pat her.

"I am alright mother. All is well. All is as it should be. I love you."

Her mother stopped what she was doing and turned around. Seeing her youngest on the floor she scooped him up into her arms and held him close with flour covered arms, burying her head into his shoulder. The little boy put his arms around his mother's neck and rested his head on her shoulder. She sobbed into his body and squeezed him tighter. Her mother would be alright, the boys would take care of her. Cassandra imagined a bag of gold coins in the cupboard at her feet. A parting gift the boy would soon find and show to his mother. Cassandra let the vision drop and curled up into a ball, hiccupping sobs into the soft pillows provided by the earth.

She must have slept, but she had no idea how long as any sense of time was blotted out by the enormous rock guarding the entrance of the cave. She sat up. The fire was still going. The glow of the unchanging embers reassured her that she was not alone.

New visions accosted her. There was fighting in the desert, a slaughter of men incapable of defending themselves against such opposition. She again saw the ships now engaged in battle.

"Now is the time."

A disembodied voice spoke. It did not really matter where it came from. Cassandra knew that she now needed to invoke the help of the Elements. She stood in the light of the fire and called out the names of those who offered their service to her.

"Chaos, if you love me, send the storms that will defeat the Queen's navy. Blow hard and crash them on the rocks. You know what to do."

"I am there, I will be with you. Come watch."

Cassandra found herself robed in purple, riding the winds with Chaos. Below, the water churned not just with ships and men, but also the Naiads fierce in their anger, turned to water demons that climbed the ships in search of men, seaweed trailing their hellish faces. The wails of men and sea sirens joined in one freakish scream.

Chaos churned the waves with his force and turned the skies black above them. Lightning streaked across the sky and set some of the ships on fire. Gaia shuddered like a dog shaking water from it's back. The world changed.

Again Cassandra woke to find herself in the comfort of her cave. She knew it was over. The Queen and her consort were both dead. There was nothing left to do. She closed her eyes and went back to sleep.

"Right. But what does this have to do with me?" thought Morgan.

"You asked the muses to show you how you know the wind. They did as they were asked."

"So, I'll play along. For fun let's say that I was some sort of seer in Egypt, for Cleopatra of all people, and then I got introduced to the Elementals."

"You are an elemental force."

"You mean now? That's hard for me to believe."

"It makes no difference to me what you believe and what you don't believe. Ask a question and you will get an answer. What you do with that information is your business. But let me ask you this, how do you feel about water?"

Morgan looked out the window toward the darkening lake. Water had always felt like a second home to her. Her parents told stories about how she hardly needed lessons to learn to swim. Her grandparents referred to her as the "little mermaid". She swam every chance she got; long distances in pools, in ponds, in lakes. She worked as a lifeguard, swam competitively through college and taught swimming lessons. *"So I have an affinity for water?"*

"It is an elemental aspect of you. Just like setting fires or…"

"I need to go check on the kids."

As Morgan got up she noticed the rain had stopped. She stepped out on the deck and watched the last of the light fade from the sky over the lake. She laughed to herself. *"So if I really can call up the wind, blow now."* Nothing. The leaves of the hemlock that arched over the railing two stories high showed no sign of movement. *"Chaos, if you are my friend and this is real, please make the wind blow."* Again, nothing. Morgan turned to go back inside. *"Ariadne, what's the point of screwing around with me?"*

"There is nothing you need. These are not forces to be trifled with just because. Ask for the leaves to wave to you, ask Chaos to simply say 'hello'."

"Sure, why not. I'm sure they are just dying to say 'hello' to me. Chaos, if you are out there please ask all these leaves to wave 'hello' to me." Morgan felt a breath of air at her neck like a lover's kiss, making her squirm with ticklish delight. She heard the chimes below the house play. The leaves of every tree as far as she could see down the hill in the declining light fluttered and flapped. Each leaf moved of its own accord conducted by the lightest of breezes. Morgan stared at the waving leaves and laughed out loud.

Day 46

"Ben, I have to know some sort of budget if I'm going to find a house for us."

"I don't think we can spend more than £2000 a month."

"You realize that £2000 a month is nothing in London. We're going to have to move way out of town. What do I do about Daisy's school?"

"You'll just have to take her on the tube from wherever we land."

"I need a budget. I need to know how much we'll have for everything so I can figure it out."

"I've told you what you need to know." Ben turned his focus back to the computer in his lap and ended the discussion.

Tears welled up in Morgan's eyes, so she turned and left the den. She went upstairs, closed the door behind her and sobbed into her pillow. Sometime later she awoke to find Daisy sitting on the bed petting her hair.

"Mommy, why are you so sad?"

"Mommy's ok, don't worry sweetie. She just has a lot of stuff to do right now, that's all. It's ok." Morgan welled up again. She sat up against her pillows and pulled the little girl into her lap.

"I hate it when you're sad Mommy…"

Morgan pressed her nose into the back of the child's hair, inhaling the scent of watermelon from her kiddie shampoo. She sniffed and hugged Daisy a little tighter. Daisy responded by hugging her tighter too. "Mommy's ok honey, don't you worry, everything's going to be ok."

"I'm going to go make you a card and some drawings, ok Mommy? That will make you feel better." Daisy hopped off the bed and headed for the open door.

Morgan felt more tears sliding down her face. She tried to keep her voice from breaking as she said, "Mommy would love that. Thank you angel." Morgan leaned down and picked her computer up off the beige bedroom rug. She got on the rental website suggested by Olivia.

"*Ariadne, I wish this was something you could help me with.*"

"*Is there some reason I can't?*" she felt Ariadne's heart hug as she flipped through pictures of apartments on the computer screen.

"*It's not spirit related.*"

Laughter tinkled somewhere in her chest and bubbled up to her ears. "*You think I am that limited? What would be the point of me?*" She sounded somewhere between bemused and irritated.

"It just didn't occur to me that you might be… I don't know. Please, if you can, just help me. I can't deal with any games."

Three green heads popped up from the foot of Morgan's bed. *"Did someone say something about games? We loooooooooovvvveeee games! What are we going to play? Let's have some fun!"* The muses bounced off of each other and the furniture never ceasing to move.

"Fun, this is not fun. This game is called: the-impossible-task-of-finding-a-house-that-doesn't-cost-the-earth-and-is-in-a-decent-neighborhood-in-London-in-less-than-six-weeks. That's what this game is called."

The green dynamos screeched to a halt. They made mooneyes at her as they peeped over the edge of the bed. She felt a pain in her chest. She sighed.

"I'm sorry guys. I need you to help me have fun with this. I am having a hard time and you're always so cheerful. When you're happy, my heart is happy."

Ariadne broke in, *"Call your landlord."*

Morgan picked the phone up from beside her on the bed and called her landlord. "Patricia, hey it's Morgan Gardiner, I was just-"

"Oh I'm so glad you called. What perfect timing. I was just about to ring you. I hope you haven't found something that starts in June. Our new tenants can't move in until August, so I hoped to extend your lease for a month. The only caveat is that we need to get a little work done in the house. What if we cut the rent in half for your trouble? Could I entice you to stay for another month?"

"Ummmm... oh, ok, yeah that could work. Sure. Thanks."

"Have you found anything yet?" she asked.

"No, not yet, still looking." Said Morgan.

"Ok well keep me posted. It sounds like this may have worked out for both of us."

"Yes, isn't that nice when that happens" offered Morgan.

"Just so. Speak soon. Goodbye."

"Bye"

"Bye"

"Bye"

"Bye," After five years in London Morgan had still not figured out why it took so long for the Brits to get off the phone. It was never just one goodbye.

Day 50

"Mama, I had a weird dream last night." Said Daisy as she clasped Morgan's hand on the walk to school.

"Did you baby? What happened?"

"A man came to see me. He had dark hair and weird sparkly eyes and a really pretty voice. He sat on my bed and talked to me."

"Was this a ghost?"

"No, I don't think so. I see them when I'm awake. This was different. Like I was awake, but not awake at the same time."

"Ok. What did he say to you?"

"He asked me about things I like. He told me I'm really special. He knew I could see ghosts like the little boy. He told me I'll be really powerful when I learn how to use my gifts. He said he wants me to help him. But I don't think I want to."

Morgan's mind reeled as they walked past the white townhouses with black iron fences native to Kensington. Townhouses that often sold for more than £10 million pounds. She wouldn't be apartment hunting here.

"Did he give you a name?"

"He said I could call him Luke. Mama I didn't really like him. He acted like he knew me really well, but he doesn't. What do I do if he comes back?"

"Oh honey, I'm sure it's just a dream. I'll see what I can find out and we can talk about it after school, ok?"

They arrived at Daisy's tony school. A stream of navy blue clad children tapped up the steps to greet the headmistress who smiled by the door. Each child stopped to greet her, shake hands and say, "Good morning". Morgan leaned over and kissed Daisy on the top of the head as she gave her shoulders a squeeze.

"Bye Mama, love you!" said Daisy as she turned to go up the steps of the converted townhouse just off Kensington Square.

Morgan walked back toward the house. *"Ariadne, who is Luke?"*

"Luke is the shadow side of a very powerful being."

"Are you telling me that Luke is a demon?"

"No. He is much more powerful than a demon. Religions cause humans to categorize things as 'good' and 'evil' when really that does not exist here. It gives them a false sense of security. We all have shadow and light within ourselves. There is a necessary balance. Nothing can be created without something being destroyed. Therefore the destructor cannot be 'bad' or 'evil' to use your terms because it is partnered with the creative force."

"Is he the Destructor?"

"Well, yes."

"Why is he talking to my daughter?"

"Because she is, or will be, a very powerful creature when she comes into her own. He needs a creative force to balance him. But right now he's likely doing it to get your attention."

"So he really wants me to balance him?"

"Yes."

Morgan reached her house. From the front door she climbed the interior stairs quickly. The computer was in the bedroom. She sat on the bed and turned it on.

"You. Are. Ready. To. Write. YAAAAYYYYYYY!!!!" The muses tumbled in from nowhere and rolled across the floor.

"Guys this is serious." Morgan said out loud.

The muses stood at attention and attempted their most serious attitude.

"No, we are not fucking around here! Help me." Morgan's hands clenched into fists.

"We will. We will. We will." They crept closer. Their bodies twitched with anticipation.

"Sorry. I'm just scared. Please help me see this life where I knew Luke before."

Her fingers flew across the keys:

"Girls we are you going?"

The three sisters froze. Their father was supposed to be in the grove checking the olives. He always did that after lunch.

"I hope you are not going to see that crazy man with the rest of the sheep today."

Issa, the oldest, was a smooth talker. "No, father, of course not. We're going to the well. We need some water."

"In that case I suggest you take some jugs."

"Of course, we were just going to get them out of the kitchen."

"Very well. You will be back before dark. And remember, little sheep stick together."

"Yes, father."

He headed down the hill without looking back at them.

"You silly goose. Water? You couldn't think of anything better than that? Now we have to carry those jugs and come back with water in them." Barbara, the middle sister, always complained.

"If it wasn't for me you wouldn't be going. We'll just take one. He knows what we're doing. He was just letting us know we weren't getting away with it," said Issa.

Mary, the youngest sister, had the lightness of being her father's favorite. She smiled at her sisters' bickering. She was just glad her father let them go. The maid told them about the man who came to town. She heard he said things that made the authorities angry. There were rumors he had special powers. He travelled with a group of people who danced and sang and seemed too happy to be real.

By the time they got to the field just outside of town a large crowd gathered. The land was flat and the man had already started talking. They were at the back. Mary could not see him as she was not tall enough to see over the backs of the people in front of her. Frustrated, she climbed a tree.

"Mary, you can't do that." Issa grabbed at Mary's clothes as she swiftly pulled herself up into the branches. A few others had done the same. She settled herself in as seemly a position as possible, tucking her dress underneath her in a modest way.

Looking out over the crowd she saw neighbors and friends from her town. Lifting her eyes she looked toward the sound of the voice, but all she could see was light. The man speaking was as bright as the sun. She felt her body shake and darkness closed around her. She fell out of the tree.

Mary woke to the sight of concerned faces closing in on her. She startled and cried out. Her sister Barbara reached out and petted her. Issa held Mary's head in her lap as she lay on the ground. Embarrassed, Mary tried to get up but was prevented from doing so. As she lay there, the crowd parted and a man in white knelt down next to her. His kinetic dark eyes were flecked with gold that shimmered as he gazed at her. He did not speak.

"Get up, come with me."

Mary sat up. Her skin danced with goose bumps as she looked into his eyes, her body flooded with warmth and a swooning joy embraced her. "Was this love?" she thought.

"Yes and no. I will explain. Come with me."

Mary realized that he did not speak aloud. She heard him in her head, "I, I can't... my father, my sisters..." In her confusion she responded to him out loud. She stared into his eyes.

Someone nearby said, "She is confused and shaken, but she is fine. She is fine." Another whispered to her sister, "Get her some water and let her rest for a few minutes. Then take her home."

The preacher patted her hand and again gazed into her eyes and said to her, but not out loud, *"I hope you will come with me. I need you to make this work."* Then he stood and made his way back through the crowd.

Mary felt like her mother had died again. She felt sick to her stomach. The warm dancing feeling left her. A seminal loneliness invaded her heart and she burst into tears. The crowd dispersed and she was left with her bewildered sisters.

When they got home the sisters reported to their father that Mary had fallen from a tree and hit her head and she was not herself.

"How could you have let this happen?" he thundered at them as he left the room to find Mary.

He found her sobbing in her room. When she saw her father she threw herself at his feet. "Please, I have to go back. I have to find him. I don't want to live without him."

"You have to find who? Who can you not live without?"

"The preacher. The man who was there. He was dressed in the robes of the sun. He shone like nothing else. His presence hit me like lightning. He spoke to me in my mind. I've never felt anything like it. I love him."

"What? This is crazy talk. No one spoke to you in your mind. You hit your head today, that is why you are acting like this. You just need some rest."

"Father, Father. I'm not crazy." She clung to his robes as she tried to prevent him from leaving. "I know what I saw. This man glowed like a thousand stars. His presence hit me like lightning and I fainted. It's why I fell out of the tree. Please listen to me. Please help me."

He yanked his robes from her grasp and left the room to find the doctor.

The doctor found Mary in the same state; wailing and begging to be allowed to go find the man who was preaching. Strict orders were given to all the servants in the house that Mary should not be allowed to leave under any circumstances. The doctor said that she had hit her head and would probably be fine in a couple of days. In the meantime, there was not much he or anyone else could do except keep her from harming herself.

For three days she refused food and only consumed water. She stopped speaking and mutely stared out of the window. Her father returned to speak to her.

"Mary, for the love of God you must eat."

"No, for the love of God I must not."

"Why would God not want you to eat?"

"Because God wants me to follow Him."

"Who, the crazy man?"

"Yes."

He stood. "Never, Mary. Never. What did he say to you? Did he tell you he would marry you? Crazy men like that take girls like you in and turn them into whores. You would never marry. Your children would be bastards. No, No, No!"

"I cannot speak to you. You will not understand."

"Would you do this to me? Would you go running off with this crazy man to be his whore and throw away the life I have worked so hard to give you and your sisters?"

"It's nothing like that. I only want to be with him. He needs me to help him. I don't know how yet, but I know I must."

"And be his whore. Never. You will rot in this room before I will allow that to happen. You have lost your mind."

195

`Mary remained silent and continued to stare out the window at the hills in the distance. Her father did not see that tears made silent tracks down her cheeks.`

Morgan stopped. She could hear herself breathing. "*Is that who I think it is?*"

"*We told you you were Jesus!*" The muses ran for Morgan's door and hurled themselves down the stairs.

"*That's not funny. Mary Magdalene? Really? The Elementals? Where are you going with all this?*" Morgan addressed Ariadne in her mind.

"*There is a theme running through all these women; the Miko, Cassandra, the Balancer, Mary... You have to figure that out. And how it applies to you.*"

"*What? That they are all women who died horribly or who were turned into whores by history? What does that have to do with anything? And what does that have to do with that Luke creature and Daisy?*"

Ariadne laughed, "*Do I need to spell this one out for you?*"

"*Are you saying that Jesus is Luke?*"

"*Luke is a shadow side.*"

"*I thought Jesus was perfect.*"

"He was a perfected soul which means he has both shadow and light in balance."

"Why is the shadow separate now?"

"That's a different story. You need to talk to Luke."

"Why?"

"Because you do not want to lose your daughter."

"Oh no, no. No! It was one thing to pretend I could change the weather or play psychic games with spirits, but, no. No, I don't want to do this anymore. I'm out. I quit all of it. I'm not even sure I believe it. I'm not going to play this game if you're going to start threatening my children. I am out. Done. I have too much shit to deal with as it is. Stop. Just stop."

"As you wish. You have free will. But know I'm always here if you need me."

"Thanks. But, no. I'm done."

Day 53

Morgan opened the front door to find Ophelia on the stoop. A black car waited for them in the street.

"Thanks for fitting me in."

"No, problem. I'm just gonna split the charges with a couple of those clients you sent my way, it's the least I can do and I have gotten paid to find you two houses so far in London."

"Thanks." Morgan's face flushed at the thought of begging for favors.

Ophelia continued as they climbed in the chauffeured black car, "It's a good thing I like a challenge -are you sure that's all we can do? Finding a place anywhere near here is going to be difficult at that price."

"I can only tell you the budget Ben gave me. Sorry."

The black car turned left on Earl's Court Road and headed away from the bustle of London central.

"I have a couple of places, but they're really small or they need some work."

Morgan looked out the window at the passing ethnic food shops that lined Earl's Court like parade goers on Mardi Gras day; eye-catching paint and foreign script told a different story. "Let's just see where we go."

They pulled up to a series of boxlike white townhouses in a converted mews behind a busy road. Morgan could touch the ceiling with an upstretched hand and the place smelled of mold. Ophelia looked at her, "I don't think we need to go any further, right?"

"Shit. I hope it gets better than this."

They got back into the chauffeur driven car, which was probably bigger than the mews house they had just abandoned. Ophelia always had a driver so she could focus on her clients and make simultaneous phone calls to landlords and estate agents. Morgan knew they did not have much time as Ophelia was essentially doing her a favor between appointments.

Some of the houses did not need more than a drive by. Most would barely house Ben and Morgan much less the kids. Morgan thought about the huge bed she had purchased in Thailand while they lived there, the tall cabinets that she had bought in Korea and the Choufa from the roof of a Buddhist temple. She realized that most of her furniture would not fit in the places they could afford. Was she going to have to buy all new furniture too? What would she do with the stuff they had? Was she going to have to trash everything they owned? Could they afford to do any of this? And what was going to happen to poor Rowena? She felt responsible for her. She would have to help her get a new job. Maybe Ben was in denial.

After a fruitless two hours, the black car pulled into Morgan's street with its gleaming white townhouses and bayfront windows.

"Morgan, don't worry, we'll find something. New stuff should come on the market next week. I will check with my contacts, but you should also scour the rental websites. Call me if you see anything interesting." She stuck her head back in the window as it rolled up and she gave directions to the driver for their next stop.

Day 55

Morgan stood at the kitchen sink slurping down a glass of wine. Heavy footsteps moved above her. She poured more wine into her glass and stuck the near empty bottle back in the fridge just as she heard Ben turn for the steps to the ground floor.

"Are you ready to go?" Ben lumbered down the stairs to the basement kitchen.

"Yep. Just tidying up here," said Morgan downing the rest of the glass.

Ben headed back up the stairs. "Daisy, Maaaax, you guys ready? The taxi's waiting for us."

"Please stop, you don't need to drink like this," said Ariadne.

She pulled the wine from the fridge to finish the bottle, put the glass in the sink and headed up the stairs.

"I told you I was out of this game," she thought.

The four of them piled into the back of the archaic looking black taxi. One of the best things about the London taxis was they could hold the whole family comfortably. Too bad the kids no longer wanted to sit in the backward facing jump seats. Morgan clambered in last pulling down the jump seat as she held the door. Better to avoid the argument in the first place.

"Battersea Park please." Said Ben.

Day 56

Morgan woke up fully clothed on top of her still-made bed. Her head felt like it had an axe through it. She was nauseous. The house was quiet. It was light outside. She checked her phone. It was 7:30am. *"What the hell..."* she thought. Sitting up made her queasier, but she desperately needed some water as her mouth felt like it was full of sand. *"How did I get so hungover?"*

As she staggered to the bathroom, images unbidden, like a slideshow, flashed through her mind. They had gone to dinner at the home of Ben's boss, Sterling Drake. She remembered getting in the taxi. She did not remember dinner or getting home. She had a flash of an altercation with Max. She saw an image of Daisy crying. Her stomach twisted again. She knelt down and heaved into the toilet. Then she lay on the cold floor of the white marble bathroom and pressed her cheek into her hand. She wept. Something bad had happened.

She needed a cold drink before she encountered anyone, so she crept down the stairs to the basement kitchen and family room. At least throwing up left her less nauseous. She needed some Advil.

Ben was stretched out on the chair and ottoman in front of the TV while the kids huddled together on the sofa under an old quilt that had been made by Morgan's great grandmother as Morgan thought, *"Why...? Oh God, what did I do?"*

Ben must have heard her coming down the stairs despite her attempt at silence. The puppy thumped her tail in the crate. Morgan bent down to open the crate and felt as though someone took another swing at her head with the axe. She managed to grab the counter next to the crate to keep from falling over. She unlatched the crate and watched Ben's feet walk to the back of the room to let the dog out into the patio. Next he grabbed her arm and took her out too, closing the door behind them.

She did not look at him. "Ben, I have no idea-"

"You have no fucking idea what you did last night? Jesus. You scared the shit out of the kids. You embarrassed the fuck out of me in front of my boss. My fucking boss. You got fucking sloshed, screamed at the kids, screamed at me, called all of us horrible names, dared Max to punch you, even told the taxi driver to fuck off. You were such a shit I thought the driver was going to chuck us out on the street."

"Oh God. Oh God. The kids?"

"You scared the shit out of them and they preferred to sleep down here rather than hear your ranting."

"Fuck," she said, tears slid down her face.

"You don't remember anything?" asked Ben.

"No, really the last thing I remember was getting in the taxi last night."

"*After downing the better part of a bottle of wine without having eaten anything all day long...*" Ariadne broke in. Morgan winced but did not respond to the internal dialogue.

"And you don't remember drinking bourbon at the Drake's?"

"Oh God, no, I don't. No wonder I feel like this."

"You deserve to feel much worse. I've never seen anything like that. I have never seen you like that. What the fuck got into you? How could you do that to me?"

"Ben, I'm sorry. I couldn't be more sorry. The kids-"

"Are going to hate you."

"What?"

"You did and said some terrible things. You scared the shit out of them."

"Fuck."

"Fuck is right." He slammed the door startling the dog. The kids would be awake now.

Morgan sat outside for a moment. When she looked up she saw Daisy staring at her through the glass door. She wept, hands pressed against the small square panes. Morgan got up and opened the door stepping just enough inside to close the door behind her. The little girl grabbed Morgan around the hips and pressed her wet face into Morgan's stomach. Morgan wanted to be sick. She picked Daisy up and sat down in a dining chair with the child draped over her while both of them cried.

"Mommy is so sorry... Mommy is sooo sorry, baby. There is nothing I can say. I'm so sorry, I love you..." Morgan repeated this over and over as she rocked Daisy.

"Mommy, you scaaaaared me." Daisy managed to get this much out before burying her face in Morgan's neck, her blouse sopping up the little girl's tears. "Mommy what happened?" She sat back and looked at Morgan.

"Mommy did a bad thing and she does not remember anything she said or did that scared you, but she wants to make sure that it never happens again. I am so sorry baby..." The little girl cried a while longer until she fell asleep on Morgan's shoulder. Morgan took Daisy up to her bedroom. Ben sat on the bed working on his computer. She lay the little girl down and put a blanket over her. Ben's eyes never left the screen.

Morgan returned downstairs to face Max. Max was defiantly embedded in a warlike video game. Morgan had not approved of this one, but Ben had over-ridden her objections and gotten it for him anyway. Max focused on the screen and ignored Morgan as she sat down next to him on the sofa.

"Max, can I talk to you for a sec?" asked Morgan.

Max responded by clicking harder on the crescent shaped controller in his hands. His knuckles whitened as he gripped the black plastic console.

"Max. I know you're mad at me. You have every right to be. I just want you to know that I was wrong and could not be more sorry about what happened last night."

Tears ran down Max's face, but he made no move to wipe them away. He remained focused on the screen in front of him.

Morgan got up to leave the room.

"You made me hit you. Why did you do that?" He asked, explaining the pain in her upper arm.

"Oh Max. I'm so sorry. I don't remember doing that."

"You don't remember? Why? Cuz you were drunk?" he asked.

"Yeah. I was drunk. I drank too much on an empty stomach. I got so drunk I don't remember even being at the Drake's, which is really scary to me. And worse, your father tells me I said really mean things to you and Daisy."

"And you made me hit you. You screamed at me until I did it."

Morgan sat back down and heaved a tearful sigh. She did not want to sob in front of Max; she bit down on her lip.

207

"I'm sorry. I know that seems a totally inadequate thing to say, but I have nothing else right now. I'm quitting drinking for the foreseeable future. I never want to do that to you again. Or your sister, or your dad."

Max continued to stare at the TV and play his game.

Ariadne cut in, *"There is pain in separation. You cannot deny yourself and expect to be ok."* Morgan ignored the voice in her head and the heart hug in her chest.

She went to a hot yoga class to try and detox her body and her mind. In dead body pose at the end of the class she dreamed of London taxis and tigers. She rode in a black taxi with her pet tiger. The tiger took up the entire space inside the driverless cab. She drove the car with her mind as she sat in the back and petted the enormous striped head that purred in her lap. Once she got to wherever it was they were going, she left the tiger in the taxi as he might scare people who did not know him. She got out and went inside. She spoke to a group of people until someone mentioned that a tiger was going crazy in a taxi outside the door. She rushed outside to find her lovely pet tiger tearing the inside of the cab apart. She opened the door to let him out. He loped out gracefully and pressed himself insistently against her legs like an oversized housecat. She closed the door to the ruined car and started to walk. The tiger calmly followed her everywhere she went.

Day 56 (later)

"I really fucked up." Morgan said into the phone while watching the puppy sniff around for the perfect pee spot on their back patio.

"What happened honey?" asked Rachel.

"I got really drunk at the Drake's."

"The Drakes? Oh shit. Isn't that Ben's boss?"

"Yeah, he's really pissed. But that's not the worst part…"

"What happened?"

"I scared the shit out of the kids. I guess I was shouting, I don't know. I made Max hit me or something. I honestly don't remember."

"Are the kids ok?"

"Yeah. I guess. Max isn't talking to me right now. Daisy spent an hour sobbing in my lap."

"Oh, honey… really it's no wonder. I mean you wouldn't be human if you didn't have some sort of breakdown. Seriously."

"But the kids-"

"But everything. I personally think you need to call Jeff or give that spirit guide, or whatever, a talking to. Or just check out of the whole thing."

"I did check out. I told the spirits I was out. Things got really weird, shit I haven't even told you about. I just need to focus on finding a place to live and what we're gonna do about school for Daisy and if we can even afford to do any of this. But apparently I'm not dealing well with that stuff either."

"You've got a lot going on honey. I think you're right. Just focus on the life stuff right now, it's enough. I'd be getting that drunk every night if I were you."

"Not if you had this hangover."

"You know, in a way, I'm really proud of you."

"Why the hell-"

"That was a huge and well-deserved 'fuck you' to Ben. I'm sorry the kids witnessed it, but fuck him."

"It would be better if I could remember it, and if the kids had not been there," said Morgan.

"Well, nothing's perfect. Please drag my ass to yoga tomorrow."

"Will do. Thank you."

"Nothing to thank me for. See you tomorrow."

"Bye honey."

Morgan let the puppy pounce into the house ahead of her. She pulled out a treat and lured the dog back into her crate for a nap. "Good girl," said Morgan, closing the latch.

"You are not perfect Morgan."

"I thought I had free will."

"You do. I'm not suggesting you do anything. I am just trying to help you understand things in a way that might make you feel better."

"That would be a miracle."

"Morgan, it is your imperfections, your human-ness, that allows your soul to learn the lessons of this life."

"Big surprise. You've lost me again."

"Revel in your mistakes and your imperfections because those are the very things that are going to make you whole in the end."

"Maybe, but that doesn't help my kids right now."

"Oh, but it does."

"How the fuck does it do that?" Morgan responded, almost laughing with surprise.

"Their souls chose you for their mother in this life because of the very lessons that they need to learn. So whatever happens, it is all part of the Universal game."

"I think that let's me off the hook a little too easily."

"It does not mean that you cannot learn something right now. Blanking out on alcohol seems to create, rather than solve, problems."

"Right. I think I know that, thanks."

"Okay, so lesson learned. Now you have to learn how to deal with all these things in your life in such a

way that you do not upset your kids or feel anxious and depressed yourself."

"Well that's where I fall down. I'm completely overwhelmed, I don't feel capable of dealing with any of this. Spirits or otherwise."

"But you are totally capable, you have all the tools you need. You just need to ask for help and then you need to think of this as play - as a giant game. All these souls are here playing a great game. It's up to you how you see it."

"Well I don't see it."

"Then let the Muses show you."

"You want me to write?"

"It's the best way for you to connect, Morgan. It's where the magic is."

Ben had disappeared with the kids. She guessed they'd gone out for an early dinner. She sat in her favorite chair and picked up the computer.

"We. Love. You." The muses somersaulted into view with each word, one at a time. Morgan sighed and smiled at them.

"Thanks guys. It's nice to know someone does." Morgan said as she blinked away tears.

They huddled at her knees, gave each other a round of high fives and announced; *"Now we write!"*

The pictures formed in Morgan's head and she typed.

It was a carnival. A crazy carnival filled with creatures she had never seen before. A squidlike form waved tentacles at her in greeting as it ran up the stairs of what appeared to be a Ferris wheel. The ride attendant spoke to the waving appendages before it sat in one of the revolving cars. The car containing the squid-being swept up toward the top of the Ferris wheel where it flipped and cast it's occupant to the blue sky above. It disappeared in a flash of light.

"I don't want to go on that ride," she thought.

"That's the point of the ride." A sparkling light body walked next to her. This presence was an animated three-dimensional cutout of a starry night sky in the shape of genderless person. "Look around."

Flashes of light popped off in the sky above the carnival like daytime fireworks. Lines of people, but not people, creatures of every type, tall, skinny, large, small, green, purple, bumpy, smooth, rabbit eared, no-eared, hairy, bald, some like sea creatures, were lined up to get on these rides only to be flung to their deaths.

"What is this place?" she asked of the person-shaped star package who walked beside her.

"It's the gateway of souls."

"Where are they going?"

"To Earth. If you watch, you see they get their instructions from the attendant before they get on the ride. They know what they are supposed to accomplish in this incarnation. They are told, but they will forget."

"Why do they forget?"

"It's part of the game. They know before they leave this place and then they have to figure out how to remember before they can come back and play again."

"Why would they want to do that?"

"Because it's how we evolve. Most of these souls waited a millennium or more to get a chance to play on Earth. It's the best classroom we have."

"What do they have to learn?"

"How to follow their hearts. That's how they remember. That's how they learn."

Morgan heard the front door open over her head. She heard the sound of the children coming in with Ben. She heard Daisy's light footsteps run to the top of the basement stairs.

"Daisy, come back and take your shoes off," directed Ben.

"Where's Mom?" asked Max.

"Probably downstairs," said Ben.

Daisy and Max tromped down the stairs. "Look Mommy! Look what I got!" Daisy held out a giant multicolored lollipop still wrapped in plastic.

"Oh my gosh, that thing's almost as big as your head," said Morgan.

"Yeah, you should have seen the candy floss we got, it was huge!" said Max.

"Where did you guys go?"

"There was a carnival in Hyde Park."

"You're kidding." Said Morgan.

"Why would I kid about that?" asked Max.

Day 58

"Ben, we have to talk about this."

"And I guess we have to do it now?"

Morgan ignored the question. "I have looked at everything in the budget you gave me within a 20 mile radius from the house. The best thing I've found is a tiny two bedroom flat in Brook Greene. That's it."

"We can't live in that."

"I know. So either you have to give me more money to work with or we have to come up with another plan. We have to be out of here by the end of next month." Morgan looked around the room and imagined all the glassware and knick-knacks and lamps and books to be boxed up. What was she thinking when she left DC? She had drug silver chafing dishes and similar useless crap with her through four countries and 6 house moves.

"I told you there's no more money. Not if the kids are going to the same schools, particularly if Max is going to boarding school." Ben set his jaw and looked at the ground.

"Then what do we do?"

"I hate this. I really hate this, but maybe you and Daisy need to move back to the States. I can stay here with Max and my job. Max can finish up Year 8 and then go on to Marlborough as planned. You guys could go back to New Orleans."

"How do you think Daisy is going to feel about that?" asked Morgan.

"She'll be ok. She knows her daddy loves her and I can come to visit a lot. It'll work out. This seems like the best plan for now."

"Assuming my parents don't mind us moving in with them."

"Are you kidding? They'll be thrilled. Once I get this figured out, we can get you a house in New Orleans. You've always wanted to have a house in New Orleans."

"I guess I better call my parents and see what they think. How am I going to get Daisy into school? What are we going to do with all the stuff?"

"We can store it."

"That costs money."

"Well you can probably get rid of a lot of stuff and then we can store what we absolutely have to. It shouldn't be much."

Morgan thought of the children's rooms bulging with stuffed animals, books and toys. The cabinets in the dining room held full sets of twelve crystal goblets for wine, twelve crystal goblets for water, two different sets of china, chafing dishes, silver water goblets, silver wine coolers, champagne buckets, dessert china, sake glasses from Japan, mother-in-law teapots from Korea, silver platters, silver tea sets, serving plates, silver serving pieces. Then there were the sofas, art, the piano, dining table, eight chairs, four beds, four armchairs. The bed she and Ben slept in had been lifted by a crane through the window, as it could not fit up the stairs. The list made Morgan tired.

"Sure. I'm sure it will be no problem for you," said Morgan.

Ben got up to leave the room. "You always manage this stuff. This is what you were made for - figuring out how to deal with this kind of stuff."

Day 61

"So you're really leaving London and moving back to New Orleans?" Rachel tucked her legs up under herself as she scratched the puppy's head. Morgan ignored the fact that the dog was not supposed to be on the sofa.

"It looks that way."

"I guess I'm not surprised that Ben suggested this, it kind of works well for him."

"Honestly, he didn't even pretend to be upset. It's almost like he planned it." Even as Morgan said them, she realized the truth of her words. Wide-eyed she stared at Rachel from her favorite chair.

"Holy shit. That makes a lot of sense. Of course that's why he wouldn't tell you about the budget or help you find a place. He wants you to move back," said Rachel.

"That also explains why he doesn't seem worried about paying for the kids' school. This isn't about money."

"Do you think he's actually losing the ex-pat package?"

"Who knows, I've never even known how much money he makes."

"Oh my God, are you kidding?"

"No."

"What about your taxes? Don't you have to sign your taxes?"

"Well, yeah, but honestly I don't think I have signed any taxes for a couple of years now. I hadn't thought of it before."

"Do you think he is forging your signature?"

"Jesus. I don't know. Maybe. Maybe I need to..."

"Figure out what *you* want, because it sure seems like he's taking care of himself."

"Wow. Yeah. Crap. How could I have been so stupid?"

"You aren't stupid. He's just browbeaten you into submission and it looks like he's found a way to have his cake and eat it too. He sends you and Daisy back to the States and Max to boarding school. Wham bam, thank you ma'am he's free and easy here in London and you are safely out of the way."

Morgan took it in. And then she surprised herself. Instead of feeling sad, she felt exhilarated - she felt like a dirigible cut loose from the binding ropes holding it to the ground. She was free. And she realized that it was exactly what she wanted. And she did not have to be the bad guy. She just had to play along with the game.

Day 62

"You're up early." Ben walked into the bedroom fully dressed.

"So are you."

"I slept downstairs on the sofa. I got in so late, I was afraid of waking you."

Morgan did not respond.

Ben sat on the foot of the bed and said, "I've been thinking about this situation. If you guys move back to New Orleans, I think we might be able to buy you a small house. We have some money saved; I don't want to waste it on living expenses here, but if we're investing it in a house, that would be different."

"Really? Just like that? I've been begging you for a budget for months. And now you suddenly come in here telling me we have enough money for a house in New Orleans?"

"I... I've been working on the numbers-"

"But you won't tell me what they are?"

"I'm telling you we have enough for a house in New Orleans."

"You're going to have to tell me more than that. I'm going to need an exact number to tell the agent in New

Orleans. I need to know if we are shopping with cash or if we need to prequalify for a loan. I need details."

"I'll have them for you in the next couple of days."

"No, I want them by the end of today, Ben. I'm tired of this. I realized I haven't seen our taxes in years. I want to know everything. I want to know how much money you make. I want to know how much I have to buy a house with."

"What's gotten into you Morgan? Why are you being such a bitch? Here I come offering you the house in New Orleans that you've always wanted. And suddenly you're accusing me of fucking around with our taxes."

"It's awfully convenient for you to have me move to New Orleans now. Don't think I don't know about Marie." Said Morgan.

"I don't know what you are talking about. I'm just trying to make the best of a difficult situation here."

"And the best you can do is to have half your family move across the ocean? What's the plan Ben? Are you going to start looking for a job in New Orleans?"

"Well, no. My job doesn't really exist there."

"So your permanent plan is for me to move with Daisy to New Orleans and you to stay here indefinitely?"

"Well, yes."

Morgan stood up. "That sounds like a divorce to me."

"I don't know what you mean. I think this works best for everyone. I work here. You get to move back to New Orleans."

"Let me make this clear. If this is what you think is best, it will be the end of our marriage, I'm going to ask you for a divorce."

"That's not where I was going with this. I don't think that's good for the kids."

"Oh and you think us living on separate continents is? You think having a woman on the side that you think I don't know about is a good plan? You hardly ever see the kids. My only real concern is Max being here in boarding school."

"I don't think we need to do this…"

"I don't hate you. I probably should be mad at you. But right now, I just want out. The first step is buying me a house in New Orleans and finding you an apartment here with room for Max if he comes in on the weekend or for short holidays. We can work out the rest later."

"Are you serious?"

"Yep. I am."

"I came up here trying to be nice. Trying to come up with a way for this to work for everyone."

"Great. I'm telling you how this is going to work for me. You're still going to get to be here in London and do whatever you want to do. Daisy and I won't be standing in your way. But I'm not going to continue to be married to you unless you want to drastically change things. Starting now."

"I'm not getting into an argument with you." He got up and walked out.

"No, you're not," thought Morgan, *"but I see where this is going now."*

Morgan sat back down on the bed. Looking out the window she saw the sun rising above the rooftops of the neighboring townhouses. Streaks of clouds shot upward as though they had been shot from a cannon. She sat for a moment watching the morning come.

Morgan heard a noise at the bedroom door. Daisy came in holding her favorite baby doll and climbed up into Morgan's lap for a cuddle. Morgan squeezed the little girl. "Baby girl, are you hungry? Would you like me to make some pancakes?"

"Pancakes? Yes! Can I help?"

"Of course."

Daisy jumped off the bed and headed downstairs to the kitchen.

After everyone had breakfast, Morgan headed out to make a late morning yoga class. She walked down Earl's Court Road toward the tube station. A kaleidoscope of ethnic markets, colors, smells and people of all types rushed back and forth against a backdrop of colorful signs in foreign languages. She turned into the tube station and almost ran into the back of a man stopped in front of her. Hundreds of people headed out of the station all at once.

The man in front of her asked a woman on her way out, "What's going on?"

"Person under the train was all I heard. They've stopped all the trains." She responded as she moved out of the station with the growing crowd.

"Well I'm not gonna make that yoga class," thought Morgan. She then chided herself for being selfish - someone likely died under the train. It seemed a fashionable way to commit suicide in London and occurred on a weekly basis. Sadness moved to enclose Morgan's mind. She tuned into the spirit channel to see if anyone was there, maybe that soul still needed some help. But no spirit reached out to her.

"Does that mean you are going to play with us??" The muses bounced into view, ping-ponging themselves against various pedestrians crowding the sidewalk in front of Morgan.

"Oops. I didn't mean to do that."

The muses stopped moving and drooped like waterlogged branches in front of her as the crowd swirled around them despite their invisibility.

"You aren't going to play with us anymore?" they chorused.

Someone bumped into Morgan. *"I don't know. I love you guys, but the rest of it is too much."*

"We looooove you too! Follow us. We. Will. Find. An. Apartment. For. You." The three muses balanced themselves like acrobats on the heads of oblivious individuals in front of her.

"Really? You could do that? For Ben? That's a game I'll play."

"Yesssssss!!!" Now the muses hopped from head to head amongst the crowd as if they were crossing a stream and trying to stay dry.

"How are we going to do that?"

"Yayyyyyyyy!!! She wants to plaaayyyyyyy!! Follow us!" As one they hopped off the heads of their unsuspecting supporters and ran ahead of Morgan, threading themselves through pedestrians as they went.

"Hey guys, wait up! I can't follow you!"

"You can't lose us! We are always with youuuuuuuuuu."

Morgan smiled and slowed down. They would come back. She headed in the direction of the house. She guessed they were playing hide and seek. In answer to her unasked question a muse popped it's head out of the doorway of a Halal market, the one with the delicious

227

watermelon and haloumi cheese. When she saw the muse, it ducked back in and disappeared. Two other muses pressed themselves against the wall of a bank on the corner, and then took off skipping down the side street behind it.

"Where are we going?"

"Wait and seeeeeeeee..."

They balanced on top of one another and moved a half block ahead of her. Then they turned down another street about two blocks off of Earl's Court Road. Morgan found herself on a street she had never seen before. It was quiet with small, neatly kept, turn of the century townhouses in bright colors. The muses stopped in front of a purple house with stone steps and bright white trim. A hand-made sign in the window said: **For Rent, 2 bedroom apt. Call 7825 733 430 to inquire**. Morgan took out her phone and snapped a picture of the house and the sign.

The muses bounced up and down the steps of the house, *"Don't wait, call right nowwwwwwww."* They somersaulted to the sidewalk from the top step as they advised her.

Morgan tapped the number into her phone.

"Hello?"

"Good morning, my name is Morgan Gardiner. I'm calling to inquire about the apartment."

"You're an American?"

"Umm, yes."

"Oh good, I love Americans."

"Thank you, that's not always the case," said Morgan with a laugh.

"Where are you?"

"Right now?"

"Yes."

"Standing on the street in front of the building with the sign."

"Do you want to see it now?"

"Sure, ok."

"I had someone look at it yesterday, but I don't like them very much. I live down the street. I'll be there in a jif."

"Ok." She hung up the phone.

"*You guys have to behave. Try not to make me laugh or this woman will think I'm crazy.*"

The muses stopped moving and stood in a line in front of Morgan trying not to twitch. Just the way they looked at her made her want to burst into fits of giggles. They looked even more ridiculous when they tried to be serious. "*Oh never mind,*" thought Morgan, "*just do whatever.*"

"*Yayyyyyy, we looooooooooooove youuuuuuuuu.*" Gravity defying balloon bounce floating ensued.

Morgan saw a woman walking toward her on the street holding a brass jail ring with keys on it. She was short and round, dressed in a royal blue kaftan that emphasized her smallness. Her gray hair was caught up in a fluffy bun on top of her head. Charm bracelets jingled on her wrist as she walked.

"Ms. Gardiner?"

"Yes."

"Oh good, I'm Flora Deddrington. Nice to see you. I can tell I'm going to like you. You have beautiful eyes Ms. Gardiner."

Morgan smiled and tried not to laugh. "Thank you."

Flora flashed a warm smile back at Morgan and laboriously mounted the steps. "Hips giving me a worry."

"I'm sorry to hear that, thanks for showing me the apartment."

"A pleasure, my dear." Flora turned, flashing a wide smile at Morgan.

Flora turned the two bolts on the door and entered the house with Morgan following. There was another door immediately behind and a staircase leading to the second floor. Flora continued, "There are two apartments here, one up and one down. Obviously the downstairs is the one that's vacant. Is it just you Ms. Gardiner?"

"Oh, please call me Morgan. Ummm, no, it's actually for my husband. I'm going back to the States with my daughter. My son will be in boarding school and only here sometimes." Morgan had not thought out what to say about the pending move. She stuttered her way through the explanation.

Flora stood in the center of a small living area that had a kitchen in the corner. White shelves and cabinets filled the opposite wall. A loveseat occupied the area under the bay window and a wooden table with four chairs stood at attention against the wall.

"Oh, I see…" said Flora. And Morgan thought she really did. "Well this is it. What does your husband do?"

"He's an attorney. Oh, uhhhh, a barrister with the Fields Corporation."

"Oh good. I like that."

"Do you mind if I look at the bedrooms?"

"Of course, there is one small and one smaller," said Flora as she stepped aside.

The room was only about two feet larger on three sides than the bed itself. A bathroom/laundry room combo then led to a smaller space on the other side with just enough room for a single bed.

"Do you mind my asking what the rent is?"

"Of course not, it's £600 a month."

Morgan could not help but catch her breath. It was a low rent for the area even if the place was small. "Oh, ok."

"I know it's low, I'm more concerned about getting good tenants than I am about making a lot of money. I have always had good tenants."

"So would it be ok if I brought my husband over to see it?"

"If he's anything like you, you are welcome to it."

"Just like that?"

"Just like that."

"Oh wow. Ok. Let me get in touch with him and I'll call you later today, if that's ok."

"Superb. I look forward to hearing from you." Then Flora cocked her head and looked into Morgan's eyes. "I'm very sorry for whatever you're dealing with. I'm sure your husband and son will be happy here."

"Uh, thanks. I'm sure it'll all be ok."

"Just so."

Morgan thanked Flora again and made her exit. The muses bounced in the street.

"Yaaaaayyyyyy, you look so happy!!!"

Morgan smiled. *"Yes, this was great, thank you for helping me. I can't believe we found this place."*

"We love yoooooouuuuuu!" Pop. Pop. Pop. They were gone.

Day 65

Morgan woke to find Daisy standing next to her bed. "Mama, he came back."

Still groggy Morgan asked, "Who came back angel?"

"The man, Luke."

Warmth shot through Morgan's legs. Ben stirred next to her. She did not remember him being in the bed when she went to sleep. "Ok baby, let's go upstairs to your room." Morgan rolled out of bed and followed the little girl out her bedroom door. Daisy's curly brown hair bounced against her short, pink nightie as she climbed the steps in front of Morgan. They both crawled into the bottom bunk in Daisy's room. "Ok sweetie, tell me what happened."

"This time I went flying with him."

"What do you mean you went flying?"

"He wrapped me up in his arms and we went to other places. We went to Tokyo and I got to watch Mia at school. I miss her."

"You went to Japan?"

"It was really cool, we were invisible and we could spy on people. We went to see Pappy and Nana too."

"In New Orleans?"

233

"No, they're at the house in North Carolina."

Morgan remembered that they had not gone back yet. She tried to control the panic she felt in her chest.

"What did he say to you?"

"He asked me if I wanted to be invisible and spy on people. I thought it sounded cool. I didn't know about the flying part until we did it. That was weird."

"I thought he scared you."

"He didn't scare me this time. But he's... he's different."

"Did he say anything else?"

"Just that he'll come back to see me again. And that he really enjoyed being with me."

"Ok..."

"Is it ok that I talked to him? I didn't know what to do."

"Sweetie, you didn't do anything wrong. I...I don't know if you should go flying with him again."

"That was fun. But I was sort of afraid I wouldn't be able to come home."

"What made you think that?"

"He asked me if I wanted to stay with him. But I told him I wanted to go home."

"What did he say then?"

"He said he hoped I might want to stay with him sometime, but that he would take me home." Daisy pressed her head into Morgan's neck and started to sniffle.

"Honey, it's ok, it's ok, Mommy will figure it out. Mommy will figure it out."

Morgan stayed in the bed with Daisy until she fell asleep. Once Daisy's breathing changed, Morgan got up and went to the chair across the room. She curled up with the comforter from the top bunk and watched Daisy sleep.

"Ariadne, I told you I was out. Why did Luke come back?"

"With you checking out of the game, Luke has even more reason to cultivate your daughter's interest."

"By scaring the shit out of her?"

"He did not have to bring her back."

"So that was a message he wanted me to get."

"Yes."

"So I can't get out of this now?"

"You can, but the Universe will find another way if you do."

"And that other way might be my daughter?"

"Possibly, or that may be Luke trying to draw you out."

"How far will he go with that?"

"Until he gets what he wants one way or the other."

"So what do I have to do?"

"Play the Game."

"How do I talk to him?"

"Meditate, set your intention to find him. He will come."

Morgan slid to the floor, her back resting against the chair. She crossed her legs and focused on her breath as it came in and out of her nose. At first it was heavy and fast, but as she observed it her breaths became softer and less frequent. She felt herself rock gently side to side. She noticed the feel of the air touching her skin, the sound of the heat as it clicked on and the quiet breathing of the child in the bed not far away.

She found herself in a garden of her mind's making. The dark green bushes struggled to contain the exuberant blossoms of fuschia, baby pink, salmon and white. The heavy weight of jasmine, sweet olive and honeysuckle filled the air around her, wind chimes tinkled in the distance. Morgan wore a loose white linen dress. She exhaled, releasing the tension brought with her from the other world. It had no place here.

A bench waited for her under the waving tendrils of a weeping willow. A stream skittered over rocks behind the engaging tree. She sat down. Now what?

A man sauntered toward her at a leisurely pace, avoiding rocks and other obstacles with an easy liquid grace as if he were dancing. Tall, lean and long legged, he wore a dark suit and a black turtleneck. When he got closer to her he looked up and smiled, a wide mischievous grin that flashed white teeth. His eyes, even from the distance, sparkled in various shades of ebony.

"May I?" he asked, indicating the other side of the bench.

"You must be Luke."

"I am."

Morgan wanted to hate him as her heart pounded, but she had to stay calm until she knew more. She wrestled with all the things she wanted to say and pinned them down her throat.

"What do you want with my daughter?"

"I don't really want your daughter. This has everything to do with you."

"Then why not leave her out of it?"

"I needed to get your attention."

Morgan was calmer than she might have been in the world outside. It was almost like a drug, that place. The very perfume of it somehow slowed things down like the scent of baking cookies. But even with the extra sense of peace, panic and fear marinated in her stomach.

"What do you want?"

Luke turned to face Morgan. "I want help." He raised both hands to his face, palms out, flexing his long white fingers that ended in an alarming length of pointed nail like cat's claws. He sighed. "I want help in your world. I need more light for my darkness and you're a very bright light. I have watched you for a long time. I'm aware that you have no idea what sort of power you possess. I can help you find that power. Your daughter is young but she will develop. Her light is already very bright. I can find darkness anywhere and everywhere these days. It isn't hard. It is almost as if I have done too well. Bright lights are much harder to find."

"What do I have to do?"

"Be willing to help me when I ask you."

"So what, am I selling my soul to you?"

Luke laughed out loud, "My minions in the religious world have done too good a job. Have I offered you a price?"

"My daughter."

"She is not yours to keep or give away."

"What do you mean by that?"

"She has free will just as much as you do."

"I'm here talking to you because you threatened my child."

"How did I threaten her?"

"You suggested she stay with you."

"And when she chose to go home, I brought her home. But she might make a different choice another time."

"What can I do to keep you away from her?"

"If you choose to work with me, I really have no need of her."

"What is it you want me to do?"

"Well you will have to find some of those powers you possess and actually use them. I am happy to help you."

"And if I don't or can't?"

"Then I just have to wait a little longer to get what I want. Your daughter has to be a little older for her gifts to come into full fruition. But I have waited a long time. Patience is one of my best qualities." As he said this a smile slid across his face and his eyes took in Morgan's. Behind those eyes she sensed a shimmer of power unlike anything she had ever experienced before. The radiance poured out of him and touched her like atomic level static electricity. She felt he could destroy anything and everything with a single thought.

"AND I COULD."

"Then why do you need me or Daisy?"

"Because destruction is not what I am after." Those words echoed in her mind as he rose and glided back across the glittering meadow. He moved with a hypnotic smoothness. Morgan watched him go. She sat for a while, her mind empty. The peace of the garden had lost its ability to soothe her. She left.

Day 75

The enormous cardboard box filled up with the contents of a life Morgan felt was no longer hers. She sat down in the dining chair and took a break from cleaning out the china cabinet. A stack of white packing paper sat at her elbow. In the box she saw the paper outlining wedding gifts of twenty years past: candlesticks, a silver chafing dish, silver serving bowls, cut crystal goblets.

Rowena walked into the room. "Ma'am I finished with the children's toys. What do you want me to do now?"

"I don't know. Take a break?"

"I can help you here." She offered.

"Okay, thanks."

Rowena reached into the cabinet and pulled out a ceramic ashtray, placed it in the center of the packing paper, and then wrapped it.

"I really don't know what I'm going to do with all this stuff. I don't even have a place to live in New Orleans yet." She sighed.

"I'll take it if you don't want it."

"Are you serious? What would you do with it?"

"I can sell it to friends or send it to the Philippines. They have great deals for shipping boxes back home."

"Really." Morgan remembered that Rowena had purchased a large home for her disabled son and mother. Rowena owned a bigger place in the rural Philippines than Morgan would probably ever live in.

"You don't want to get rid of all of it do you?"

Morgan sat up. "Actually, yeah I do. At least a lot of it. I have no idea what to do with it all. I hate to just throw it away."

"Oh please don't do that. I'd love to have it." Rowena's eyes met Morgan's and a big smile brightened her already friendly face.

"Great. Let's start sorting stuff. For one, I think you can have everything in this box if you want it."

"Really? You mean it?"

Morgan smiled back, these things meant more to Rowena than they ever had to her. "Yes, I do."

"Can I get some friends to come over and help me pack and move this stuff?"

"Of course. I'm going to go through and figure out what I want to keep. You can have first dibs on anything I don't. Sell it to your friends, give it away, make some money, I don't care. Just make it all go away."

"Yes ma'am. I will. We can have it all out of here by this weekend."

Now it was Morgan's turn. "Really?"

"Yes, you have no idea. My friends will be so excited."

"That's great. Thank you."

"No, thank you ma'am! I need to go call some of my friends to help." She put the carefully wrapped ashtray into the box and went into the kitchen.

Morgan looked around the dining room. "*All I want is the table and chairs, the Meiersdorff glasses, and my grandmother's sterling silver place settings. The rest of it can go.*" Morgan felt light enough to float to the ceiling. She loved the idea that Rowena wanted the stuff and Morgan did not care what happened to it. "*Oh I guess I better clear it with Ben first...*" she thought.

It was rare that she called Ben during the workday. He picked up. "What's up? Is everything okay?"

"Yeah everything's fine. I just needed to ask you what you want for the apartment? I am here packing stuff up and Rowena is happy to take a lot of it, which will save us moving it or storing it. I just need to know if there is anything in particular you want."

"Right. Uhhhhh... I guess I just need some pots to cook in, some utensils, some plates and stuff. You know, enough stuff for me and Max to do what we need to do."

"So, are you ok with letting the crystal and other stuff like that go?"

"Yeah, I don't really see myself using that stuff. So if you don't want it, I don't care what happens to it."

"I guess you don't," thought Morgan.

"Okay, I'll pull some stuff for the apartment. Figure out what I want and give the rest to Rowena."

"Sounds good to me. See you later or... I don't know, not sure when I'm coming home."

"Okay, that's fine." Morgan hung up the phone. She could hear Rowena in the next room speaking in rapid fire Tagalog with the usual giggles interspersed in the conversation. Rowena was excited. Morgan was relieved.

Morgan drifted between waking and sleep as another story unfolded. She opened her eyes to find three green creatures shushing each other as they tiptoed around the edge of the bed. Before they could say anything she picked up her computer and wrote everything down as images flashed in her head.

That night under the cover of darkness she slipped past the maid who had fallen asleep outside her door. The watchman at their gate slept as well. She felt a tinge of guilt for the treatment they would receive at the hands of her father when her escape was discovered. But she could not worry about that now. She had to find the man.

Several days ago she would have been frightened to be alone on the road at night. She knew very well what danger lurked outside her gates. Unescorted and unknown it would be assumed she was a whore or a leper. She preferred to be thought a leper.

She walked. She had taken nothing with her. At sunrise she found women at a well and begged for a drink of water. It would be a long hot day on the road.

"Child, why are you alone?"

"I was treated cruelly at home and forced by my father to leave. I have no wish to burden anyone. I have family in Nazareth, so I'm going to find them if I can get there before my father finds me."

"You cannot be on the road in the day without water. I have a barn where you can sleep today. Then, when it is cooler at night, you can walk."

"That's very kind of you." Mary sat down next to the woman and said nothing more. She simply stared into space. The women around her whispered that she must have undergone a very great trauma. She seemed to be a walking corpse.

Mary followed the woman in silence. She collapsed on the sweet smelling hay and fell asleep. When she woke she found a plate of bread and honey next to a cup of water. She ate and drank. A packet of bread and a skin of water were also sitting there. She took them and rose to leave. She wished to thank the woman, but the house was dark. She left.

She heard from another group of women that the man preached a little farther up the road and went in that direction, finding places to sleep during the day and moving at night despite the added danger.

The second day she noted from her hiding place that there were many more people moving on the road. This was to be a large gathering. She was not sure what she was going to do, but she knew she had to find him.

A crowd gathered on the edge of a town in a field. Mary heard people talking. Her heart felt light when she thought of him and his words, *"Get up. Come with me."*

In a daze she saw him again in white, blazing like the sun at the front of the crowd. She stumbled forward tripping and catching herself, the lack of food, water and sleep catching up with her. She only saw the light and she moved toward it. She stepped on people seated on the ground in her frenzy. She was dirty and her clothes unkempt. She looked wild. People moved away from her or shifted themselves to accommodate her movement. Aghast, they waited to see what the preacher would do.

He watched her. Then as she neared the front of the crowd he came forward to catch her just as she collapsed. He picked her up and cradled her in his arms. As he held her, he called out, "Peter, Michael. Come here." Two men stepped forward. "Take her to the landlord's house. Cool her off. Get her something to drink and eat." He handed Mary to Peter and turned back to the waiting crowd.

"You see that young woman. Seven days ago she saw me outside of Magdala. She truly saw me. She saw me with her heart. She has defied her father. Left her home and family and everything she knows. She has risked her life to follow her heart.

Unless you are willing to do this you are not truly in love with the Creator around and within you. When you feel the pull of that purest love there is nothing you would not do to hold it. There is no loss too great, no sacrifice too much, no pain that could match the pain you feel in separation from the Divine Source of Love. It is a passion without end, all consuming. This is devotion. This woman has had eyes to see and a heart open enough to feel what I offer in connection to that Source. There is no better example I could set. She is a believer, she sees what can be." He turned and left to follow Peter and Michael into the house.

The landlord intercepted him just past the door. "Who is this girl? What have you to do with her? I cannot have you bringing young unmarried girls in here. Am I to become a brothel?"

"Does this woman appear to be a prostitute?"

"No, she seems like a young girl who has lost her mind. I do not want my daughters to associate with her."

"Then you will find that you do not associate with me."

"Why Master would you say such a terrible thing?"

"Because without faith we have nothing to talk about. You either have faith in me or you do not. How do you judge the other women in my company?"

"I assumed they were married to some of the other men with you. But this girl is different."

"Where is the girl?"

"Here I will show you."

"Do I need to prepare to leave this place?"

"No teacher. I trust you. I just hope...well nevermind."

The Teacher walked in and found Mary seated with the other women sipping on a cup of water. The cup fell out of her hand as she threw herself at his feet.

"Teacher forgive me for hesitating the first time I saw you. I have been in anguish. I only ask that you let me stay in your company and serve you."

"It is not me you would be in service of. It is the God of Love. You will be in service to Love."

"Please. It's all I want."

"Get up little one." He kissed her on the forehead. It looked as though she might faint again. He caught her and helped her to sit. Crouching at her feet he took her hands and looked into her eyes, "You have done well. Your great heart has brought you back to me. You will be with me always. You are an example to all." He kissed her hands and went out to finish preaching.

Morgan sighed and looked out the window over the roofs of the nearby townhouses, watching the sky change with the colors of dawn.

Day 80

The house was filled with Filipina ladies shopping and haggling over bric a brac, silver pieces, ceramics, crystal bowls, flutes and goblets, serving trays, tea sets. Morgan could have started a catering business with all the stuff she had packed and repacked through four foreign countries. Morgan's sense of relief increased with each piece that left the house. Why had she ever felt such an obligation to keep this stuff she did not even like? Morgan no longer cared, whatever tether had held that sense of duty to those things gifted to her at the time of her marriage had been severed. She felt like a ship sunk under the weight of its cargo now slowly becoming more buoyant as the weight holding it down left piece by piece. She could imagine a time where the ship might be light and free to sail wherever it chose.

The muses had a fine time. They encouraged her to write when she could, popping out of moving boxes and playing hide and seek amongst the rubble of Morgan's life. She did not mind.

The movers were arranged, what remained in the house was about to be packed up. Rowena had lined up a new job. But Morgan still had nowhere to live on the other side of the ocean. It would take about 8 weeks for her container to make it across the Atlantic, but she had no idea where it would be unloaded.

Morgan's phone rang.

"Morgan?"

"Yes, this is she."

"Charlotte, about that house you were interested in. You know the one with the higher bid?"

"Oh yeah. What happened?"

"You know, this is unusual in a hot market, but the day before the inspection the buyer just pulled out. So, if you want to put an offer in on it, now is the time. You know the market is crazy here right now."

"Yes, absolutely. I know we do. Let me call you back."

Morgan put the phone down and saw her little green muses were back.

"You can write now! Yay!!! We love you. See everything is going to be A-OK!!!"

The usual bouncing, spinning and other-worldy acrobatics followed this pronouncement.

"It's easy for you to say..."

All movement stopped and they landed one on top of the other like a three-layered green sandwich. They looked at her with pleading eyes.

"You guys, you're so easily wounded. I know you love me, you make me so happy when I see you. Try not to listen to me too much."

Three alien balloons rose from the bed. *"You need to write it down, to make it happen. Make. It. Real."*

"What do you mean?"

"Write. It. Down. Make. It. Real." Each muse said a word and struck a pose then switched to a new pose with a new word.

"You're saying if I write it down, it will happen?"

"Yes! Yes! Yes!" One. Muse with hands on non-existent waist. Two. Muse on one knee hand outstretched. Three. Muse three seated on knee of Muse two looking flirtatious.

"Ummm... ok."

Morgan opened her computer and pulled up the realty company website. She got the address of the house she wanted to buy. Then she opened a new document.

I want to live in the house on 331 State Street in New Orleans. The owners will accept the offer we make. I am going to live there with my daughter and son where we will be very happy. I have no idea how I am going to pay for this or how it's going to happen, but my muses told me to write it down and make it so, so I thought it was worth a try.

"Yayyyy!" The muses pretended to blow horns in celebration. Then they popped like balloons and disappeared.

Morgan's phone rang again. It was her father. She picked up the phone. "Hello dearest and darling, how are you?"

"Hey Daddy, I'm ok. Just trying to get things packed for the movers."

"Well that's one of the things I wanted to talk to you about."

"Ok."

"We got a call from Charlotte a little while ago and she said that the house we put a bid on and lost is going back on the market."

"Right."

"I want to help make sure you get the house this time. I'm going to give you the money for it and then we'll work out an official loan to pay me back. I know things are tight right now, so I don't want this to slip through our hands again."

"Uh. Wow, Dad, I don't know what to say, that's a very generous offer. I guess I need to talk to Ben about it."

"Sure. But you want this house right?"

"Yes, yes I do."

"Good. As I just directed Charlotte to start writing up a cash offer on it. I'll have her call you when we get word back or if they counter. But I don't think they will. I'm offering them above list and cash. They won't get a better offer."

"I can't imagine they will, Dad. I hardly know what to say."

"Well, it's just a loan. I need the money back, but we need to stop pussy footing around here and get this done. You need a place to live."

"Thanks Dad. I'll tell Ben. Hopefully this'll motivate him to get the finances in order so we can set up a loan to pay you back as soon as possible."

"You do that. I'm sure he has the money, but he needs to figure out how to get it into a bank here as soon as possible."

"Yeah. I know. I'm sorry."

"Don't be sorry. Just get him on the job."

"Will do. Thanks Dad."

"I love you Morgan, everything's going to be ok. We're looking forward to having you back in New Orleans."

"I love you too Dad. Thanks." Morgan touched the red dot to end the call. Three muses leaned against the wall opposite her bed oozing "I told you so".

"Nice job guys." Morgan smiled.

Day 85

Morgan did not hear the sound of feet on the floor above her. Morgan headed up to the third floor to get the kids going. Max met her at the top of the steps.

"Well done, Maxie! You're already dressed for school. Daisy's still in bed?"

"Yeah. Maybe she's sick or something." He headed past her down the steps. "I'm going to get some cereal."

"Ok," said Morgan as she opened the door to Daisy's room. Daisy was splayed out as usual taking up the entire bed with her small body. "Angel," said Morgan as she sat down on the edge of the bed next to her, "it's time to get up baby. Are you feeling ok?" Morgan touched Daisy's forehead to check for fever. It was cool. But Daisy did not stir.

"Baby." Morgan kissed her on the forehead and shook her gently. No response. "Baby girl. Wake up angel." Morgan rubbed her arm and then lifted it holding her hand. It dropped to the cover as dead weight. "Baby?" Morgan felt her neck. There was a pulse. She was breathing, but she did not respond. "Angel, angel. Wake up. Daisy. Wake up!"

Rowena appeared at the door.

"Call an ambulance. Something's wrong with Daisy. I can't wake her up." Morgan turned her attention back to the child. She rubbed her hands and legs. She shook her. Nothing. She checked her breathing again. Her chest rose and sank in rhythm. She checked her pulse again. The heartbeat was strong. She checked her forehead for fever.

Morgan heard the sound of a siren approaching. Rowena stood staring at the bed. "Rowena, go let the ambulance guys in and call Ben."

Rowena turned and ran down the stairs. Morgan heard the sharp knocks of the paramedics, then voices in the hallway. A tall man with dark hair filled the door to Daisy's bedroom. He carried a box. "What's wrong?"

"I don't know. I can't wake her up. She just won't wake up."

"Lemme take a look." He knelt down next to the bed and Morgan shifted to the side. Two more guys came in. Morgan held on to Daisy's foot while the men examined her. They checked her pulse, her airway, her pulse oxygen. They attached several monitors to her.

"Any chance she got hold of some drugs?"

"Hey Mom, what's wrong with Daisy?"

Morgan got up and guided Max out of Daisy's room. "I just can't wake her up. Max, did anything strange happen last night?"

"No, I don't think so."

"Daisy didn't get into any medicine or anything that you know of did she?

"No, Mom. I don't think so. She doesn't do stuff like that, she's not a baby."

"I know. I just had to be sure nothing weird happened, like she had a headache and got something by mistake."

"No, she would've told you."

"Ok, thanks honey."

"Is she ok?"

"Um. Mrs. Gardiner?" interrupted one the paramedics.

Morgan turned to go back into Daisy's room. She heard Rowena talking softly to Max as she led him down the stairs.

"We're gonna bring the stretcher in and take her to the hospital. We're gonna need to run some tests."

Morgan knelt next to Daisy on the bed and held her hand. "Can I go with her?"

"Of course. Mac's gonna stay here with you and Daisy. We're gonna get the stretcher."

"Ok." Morgan put her head on the bed next to Daisy's prone form. "Please wake up baby." Tears slid onto the mattress.

By the time they loaded up the ambulance, Rowena returned from taking Max to school. Morgan saw her as she got in the back. "Thanks for taking Max. Please call Ben."

"I did. He said he would meet you there."

They closed the doors.

Day 86

Morgan sat next to Daisy's bed. Monitors blinked and beeped to note that Daisy still breathed and that her heart still beat. A tube in her arm kept her hydrated. The tests showed nothing unusual, there was no reason for her to be in a coma. And no one could explain why.

"Ariadne, does this have anything to do with Luke?"

"Yes."

"Where is she?"

"She is in the No Place."

"What the hell is the No Place?"

"It is a place between realms, where you found Luke before."

"In my meditation garden where I met him before?"

"Yes."

"Can you help me?"

"No. You need to talk to Luke."

Morgan folded her legs under her as she sat on the pink plastic sofa next to Daisy's inert form. She closed her eyes, took in a deep breath and called the garden to mind. She remembered the willow tree over the brook with the bench.

"Luke! Where the hell are you Luke?"

"How very charming. Is that how you get all the men?" Luke sauntered around from behind the tree and stepped over the water flowing beneath it.

"Luke. Give. Me. My. Daughter. Back."

"She's not yours. She never was."

"What the hell does that mean?"

"All souls have free will. She freely gave herself to you when she entered this life. If her soul has chosen to take a different path now, it is not yours to decide."

"She's a child."

"She's a very old soul. Not one easily commanded."

"Where is she?"

"Morgan?" Daisy's voice came from behind Morgan.

Morgan turned to see a beautiful young woman standing in front of her. Daisy, if someone had pressed a fast forward button by about ten years.

"Angel, is that you?" Morgan moved toward her.

"Yes. I suppose I should still call you Mama. But that's not really the case here in this place."

"What? Why wouldn't you call me Mama?"

"This is the eternal part of me. We have played many roles over time, you and I. I have been your daughter, your mother, your husband, your mentor."

"You mean in different lives?"

261

"Yes."

"So you've left Daisy's body?"

"For the moment. I'm trying to decide what I want to do now."

"You don't want to come back?"

"I have to decide if I can do more here or there at another time."

"What changed? Was it Luke who convinced you to stay here?"

"No. He explained some things to me, reminded me of things my soul had forgotten."

"Why am I here as Morgan and not as my soul?"

Luke responded from behind her. *"You have not disembodied. You have not chosen to leave. You are only a visitor to this place."*

"Can Daisy come back if she wants to?"

"She has free will. Her body is still functioning. It's her choice at this point."

"When does it no longer become her choice?"

"If she stays out of her body too long it will begin to deteriorate for lack of a life force. She will be unable to return," said Luke.

"Daisy, sorry - is it ok to call you that? I don't know what else to call you."

"Daisy's fine."

"Daisy, I love you. I can't imagine life without you. Is this what you want?"

"I love you too, but I am not sure this is a life I want to remain in at this point."

"Why? Because I got drunk once? Because your father and I are probably getting a divorce?"

Daisy laughed. *"No Mama. It just seems I may be able to do more here with Luke. It's just another path."*

"I don't see it that way. I see him using you to get what he wants. You're a beautiful light. But he has done something to interrupt the natural order of things. This is wrong. Don't believe him. Come home, please, before it's too late."

"I'll think about it Morgan." Luke appeared beside her, took her hand, leading her away. She turned after a few steps. *"Come back in two days."*

"Does she have two days?" asked Morgan.

"Just." Said Luke.

Morgan inhaled and opened her eyes. Daisy's motionless body lay in front of her with machines beeping.

Ben walked in with a doctor behind him. He sat next to Morgan.

The doctor checked the machines and then turned to them. "So far we've not detected any brain activity. I'm sorry to tell you but it appears she is brain dead."

Morgan's breath caught in her throat. Ben was silent. Morgan stood up and took Daisy's hand.

"She's not on a ventilator. There's no machine to turn off."

"No, but we will very soon need to make a decision about hydration and nutrition."

"Are you honestly suggesting that we let my daughter starve to death?"

"Well…"

"Get out. Get out of this room. Don't bring that up again. It's not up for discussion."

The doctor looked at Ben and then turned and left the room. Ben followed her.

Morgan reached for a chair behind her and pulled it closer to Daisy's bed. She sat down without looking and held Daisy's hand. Tears slipped down her face as she leaned over the rail and stroked Daisy's head. Then she sobbed. She let go and gave into the fear and sadness, gasping sobs over Daisy's pillow.

The warmth started in her chest. Ariadne. The feeling filled her like warm honey. *"You are loved. You are love. You are loved. You are love."* Ariadne repeated those six words so many times that Morgan lost count. Morgan's hiccupping sobs eased and finally she took a deep breath.

The warm feeling stayed even when the words stopped. *"Ariadne, what does Luke want me to do?"*

"You learned this lesson with Telemon."

"You've got to be fucking kidding me, I'm supposed to love him?"

"Yes. It's the only thing that will save Daisy."

"So I have to sell my soul to the devil?"

"That is an archaic notion and you are smarter than that."

"So what do I do now?"

"Write. Write it down. Write what comes to you." answered Ariadne.

The muses appeared in surgical masks which almost made Morgan laugh. They were respectful and reflected Morgan's mood in every other way, no bouncing, and no games.

"We want to help you, to help Daisy." They approached Morgan with sad eyes and stood in front of her on the gleaming white linoleum floor.

"I don't think I have anything to write with." As she said this she saw her bag sitting on the floor with the computer sticking out of it. *"How did that…Oh never mind, thanks guys."* She opened it in her lap.

The muses hopped up onto the pink plastic hospital sofa and she found herself in a movie as she wrote without thinking.

"Luke I want to make a deal with you." The two of them stood in the space of nothing as if suspended in time.

"Interesting, what are you offering me?"

"My love."

"Really? I don't believe it. I feel no sort of love from you. You despise me. How can you change that?"

"I can't, but I can offer you my heart. You wanted me to help you, I'm saying I will."

"It doesn't work unless you offer yourself to me unreservedly - your whole being. I need all of you."

"I'm telling you what I can give you, in exchange for Daisy."

"Daisy doesn't hate me."

"But I know you want me more. Take my heart." Morgan reached into her chest and pinched off a piece of her heart. She placed it in the palm of her right hand and held it out to him.

In an instant he changed into a gigantic beast of a man with ram's horns embedded in his skull. His skin glowed a dark red, but the long black pointed fingernails were the same. He laughed and reached out to take the piece of Morgan's heart pincer-like. *"I accept."*

Tilting his head back he held the morsel high above his mouth as if it were the most rare and delicious of treats. Just before he dropped it in Morgan felt warmth in her chest and looking down she saw within herself a sparkling and glowing heart. Luke's eyes were closed so he did not see that the nugget he was about to consume had begun to glow too. He dropped it into his mouth.

A smile formed at the edges of his lips in anticipation before he choked and gagged. *"What did you do?"*

"I gave you some of my light. That's what you wanted wasn't it?"

He gagged in response, finally spitting the glowing piece out where it lodged itself back in Morgan's chest.

"You will regret tricking me."

Morgan came out of her writing trance to the sound of alarms going off. Before she could put her computer down half a dozen people rushed into the room and checked Daisy. As a nurse pulled Morgan out of the room, she heard the words, "Cardiac arrest…"

She pressed her face to the glass and watched the doctor and nurses working on Daisy. *"Did I do this?"*

Another nurse pulled her away and left her in a waiting room. Ben came in at some point and sat across the room from her. Rachel came and held her hand. Morgan lost all sense of time.

A doctor came in, "I'm so sorry…we have no idea what happened…"

Morgan felt her throat constrict and heard her voice yelling, "No. NO. NO. NOoooo…" Rachel put her arms around her. Ben sat stone-faced in the chair. Morgan looked at the doctor who stood waiting to be asked a question. "Can I go see her?"

"Yes, of course." Morgan stood. Ben and Rachel moved as if to go with her. "No, I need to be alone with her." They continued standing but did not move to follow her. The doctor took her back to Daisy's room where all the monitors were now silent. The IV was gone. She looked like she was sleeping. Morgan sat down next to the bed and took Daisy's hand.

"I did this. I tried to trick Luke and I did this. Now I've lost Daisy." Thought Morgan.

"You can fix this," responded Ariadne.

"Oh God. I'm really sick of your shit. How the hell am I gonna fix this? My daughter is dead."

"Have you learned nothing? You can set fires at will, communicate telepathically, send spirits to the light, change the weather - have you not learned that what you call reality is not real?"

"I can't fucking raise the dead."

"Not like you think, but you can."

"Fuck you. I don't believe any of this bullshit. It was all fun and games while we were fooling around with spirits and shit, I almost started to believe that I could do all that stuff, but now... now I see it's all bullshit. And I've lost my daughter. Fuck you. Go away and leave me the fuck alone. I mean it this time. Fucking leave me alone."

Morgan sat with Daisy until they came to take her away. Ben and Rachel had come in. Morgan's head swam. Rachel and Ben steered her home. Rachel found a sleeping pill from an old prescription and made Morgan take it, then put her to bed. Ben went to tell Max.

Morgan drifted. A movie played behind her eyes as she floated between waking and sleep:

A beautiful queen sat on her jewel-encrusted throne. The only other creature in the room was a crabbed goblin with a crooked back and a bald head, except for three strands of hair combed across her forehead. Morgan listened to their conversation:

"What can make me beautiful?" asked the Goblin of the Queen.

"Why nothing so far as I can see, you are crooked and green and rough, there is none who could love such stuff."

"But surely one as powerful as you, if you loved me I could be beautiful too."

Haughty laughter echoed out through the halls, "There is no one as powerful as that, as wondrous as my beauty be, there is nothing that could change you to me!"

And the Goblin crawled away only returning each day to ask the same question of the Queen.

And much time passed and nothing changed.

The Queen grew quite tired of the endless daily exchange and made a request of the Goblin, "Bring a mirror, so you can finally see just what it is that preventeth thee from being beautiful."

So the Goblin scuttled over with a mirror in her hand doing everything in her power not to sneak a glance, fearing more than anything what she might see. The imperious Queen held the mirror high requiring the Goblin to stand and stretch her limbs for the very first time.

"Look now! I tire of this game. Look now and feel all the shame that bears down upon you. Look at what I have been forced to see all these many years whenever I am required to look upon thee!"

And so the Goblin looked, and gazed and stared some more, and before long the Goblin's eyes became wide with wonder and she stood a little taller and straightened up her back and with her delicate green hands she stroked the three tiny strands of hair that fell across her face. And soon she began to laugh and then to dance with grace. As she capered out the door, she turned to look at the proud Queen once more and blew her a gentle kiss, "I am only sorry that you never ever had me look before."

The Queen sat back amazed, the mirror resting in her lap. "How can it be? What has taken place? There is nothing as ugly in this world as that creature, I am sure!" Content not to think long on it, she soon picked up the mirror and turned the reflection on herself.

"What can have happened? What is this here? Have I become cursed? This is a trick! I know not how that demon has done this!"

Throwing the mirror down it smashed into many pieces and though she tried very hard not to look intently at each little shard, she did not succeed for each reflected something most unholy; she kept on looking as if looking would reflect a different thing, but each bit told the very same story:

I am you and you are me, if Goblin I am, so you be!

Day 87

Morgan woke to a silent house. Out of habit she picked up her computer to write down the images she had just seen. Three solemn muses stepped out from the shadows of her room. She sighed. *"Okay, you can stay, but please don't talk to me right now."* They sat on the floor next to her bed like obedient puppies. Morgan finished and put the computer back down. The heaviness of the pill drew her back under the covers; she wanted only to escape in sleep.

Memories flashed like a pictographic merry-go-round: Daisy as a baby. Daisy holding her favorite duck in the tub. Daisy on her first day at school in Japan. Daisy in her uniform in London. Daisy skiing. Daisy laughing. Daisy playing. Daisy crying. Daisy. Daisy. Daisy. Daisy. The pictures changed as she watched: Morgan the sacrifice to the warrior, Morgan dressed as a geisha, Morgan with her priest lover, Morgan learning the secrets of the book in Egypt, Morgan falling at the feet of the Beloved, Morgan walking across a sparkling meadow with an easy liquid grace wearing a black suit...

She sat up panting, adrenaline warmed legs at the ready for flight. *"I am all of these things, these people.*

They're all me, even Luke…" She remembered Ariadne's words, *"Luke is the shadow side of a very powerful being."*

"Ariadne, I'm sorry. Please just answer one question. Is Luke the shadow side of me?"

"Yes."

"Ok. I think I'm beginning to see what you're talking about. I have to learn to love myself - all of me, my shadow side. But it's too late…"

"Why?"

"Because Daisy's gone."

"You have seen Luke's power. If you believe in it, then you should believe in yours."

"That seems impossible."

"Nothing is impossible."

"Then what do I do now?"

"You already know the way."

"Who am I?"

"You are Luke, the devil, the darkness, the light, love, the other, you are Morgan, Cassandra, Cai the Miko, Magdalene, the Balancer, the goblin and the Queen…"

"Am I?"

"Get up Morgan and go look in the mirror."

Morgan rolled over and slid off the bed on the bathroom side of the room. She switched on the light as she stepped in the doorway and faced the mirror. Her

273

heart contracted and her breath stopped. The image of Luke stared back at her. No matter which way she turned, Luke's image followed her movements exactly. Looking down, her hands were her hands, there were no long black pointed nails, just her usual super short squared edge nails attached to the hands she had always known. But the image in the mirror was that of her enemy.

"Or maybe not," she thought. *"maybe not."*

She watched as the image shifted. First it transformed back to a picture she recognized as herself, then Luke again, and then she grew horns and a beard *"very funny"* she thought. Her appearance changed again and she saw her grandmother, an old man she did not recognize, the muses, a raven, the Miko, Cassandra the Seer, the Magdalene… all these creatures came and went in the mirror and each moved with her, laughed as she did, opened and closed their mouths when she did, blinked when she did, cried when she did. The images began to shift faster and faster until they were a blur of constant motion and out of the fuzzy picture emerged the likeness of Morgan.

Morgan had no idea how long she stood in front of the mirror. She felt her feet on the floor. Silence roared in her ears. She became aware of herself in her bathroom staring at her own face. *"Of course…"* she thought.

"All of these creatures are simply manifestations of me. Even Telemon and all the spirits, the guides, the

muses, even Luke. And if that's true then can I bring Daisy back?"

"Go sit. Go meet Luke in the Garden." Said Ariadne.

Morgan sat cross-legged on her bed leaning against the pillows. She closed her eyes and took a deep breath in through her nose, and exhaled through her mouth taking care to slow the breath down as much as possible. She felt her heart beating, but she knew if she could slow the breath, the heartbeat would follow too.

After a few breaths she called to mind the garden with the bench and the willow tree. She found herself again in the white dress and searched for Luke.

"*Call him. Sit down.*" Instructed Ariadne.

"*Luke!*"

"*Now sit. He will come.*"

She sat on the slight rise of a hill near the bench, crossed her legs and closed her eyes. She knew when Luke arrived. Her eyes fluttered open to reveal the dark, handsome version of Luke facing her, long legs folded in a comfortable Lotus position, one she had not been able to master. His black kaleidoscope eyes gazed at her in a bemused and quizzical way like a lover who knows you too well, but is going to let you make a fool of yourself anyway.

"*What can I do for you?*"

"*I know who you are.*"

"Do you now?" his chin snuck forward as he held her gaze.

"What is it you want from me?" she asked.

"I want you to love me."

"Why, why do you need me to love you?"

"Because I love you and it breaks my heart that you hate me so. It makes me hate myself."

As he said these words he morphed into a multi headed being with long thin necks like snakes, attached to a ribbed, funneled body that oozed a slimy, snotty substance. The contorted creature contracted as if it were in pain from the middle. The funnel tipped up in the contraction revealing something bulbous and raw. The thing writhed in Luke's place, one-eyed necks bobbed and weaved over the funnel body that could not seem to be comfortable no matter which position it took. Morgan loathed it. Morgan feared it.

"Come sit in my seat." Luke's voice now squealed with a pig-like quality.

"What?"

"Get up. Sit where I'm sitting. Take my place, see what I see, feel what I feeeeeeel." The strained voice of the distorted Luke-thing was barely able to get the words out.

Morgan got up and sat in the creature's spot. But instead of switching places, she found she embodied the oozing snake-necked mess. She felt cramped and hideous. She saw herself across the grass and was shocked at her own ethereal beauty. *Is that really what I look like?* She contracted with violent stabs in her midsection as she gazed in wonder at the image of herself.

The Morgan across from her asked again, *"What is it you want from me?"*

The Luke-Morgan beast responded, *"I want you to love me."*

She saw the look of revulsion that crossed Morgan's face. She noticed for the first time all the anger Morgan held back and how it made her seem haughty. *But it's not me, I am in pain. I am in so much pain."*

The Morgan facing her asked, *"If I could love you, how would that make you feel?"*

"Oh, oh, I would know that I am worthy of love, I would feel beautiful, fulfilled, happy. I would feel aaaaadeeeequaaaate..." tears filled the Luke creature's eyes and spilled down it's many necks.

"Change back." Said Ariadne.

Morgan was in her own body again looking at the slimy, bobbing heap. The necks sat drooped and immobile on top of the funnel shaped body. It did not move. It looked dead.

Morgan sat. Then almost without thinking she pressed a hand into her chest and withdrew a glowing crystal, which she held out to the nine-necked monster in offering. At first it did not respond. Then one of the eyes attached to one of the necks flicked open and took in the sight. As one all the necks lifted and reared back in disbelief. Morgan was not sure where its mouth was or if it even had one, so she simply held the glowing rock in her outstretched hand.

"This is my heart. I offer not a piece, but all of it to you. It is all I have, but if it will make you well, it is enough."

The funnel body reared up and vacuum-like sucked the crystal from Morgan's hand. Luke stared back at her again.

"Are you my friend now?" Morgan asked.

He smiled. *"Come sit with me. Feel what it is like to be me now that you have given me all of your love."*

Morgan got up and shifted across toward Luke and sat in his lap. Instead she found she inhabited his space and now faced the empty seat where she used to be.

"How does that feel?" His voice was still in her head.

She closed her eyes and allowed herself to feel the form of the new Luke-Morgan. She felt a deep happiness that started in the lower part of her body and rising. She felt giddy with joy. They laughed out loud together as one. She hugged herself with a childlike grip, never wanting the merry-go-round to end.

"Will you always be with me now? Will you help me?" Asked Morgan.

"I have never left you. I have always been here, but your love has transformed me. Your love binds us together as it does all things. I have loved you always since before the beginning of time. Now there is no more separation. It is the division, the separation which causes pain."

"Since this is sort of me talking to me, I already know this?"

Luke laughed. *"Yes, I guess now I am just another voice in your head."*

"But what about Daisy? Where is she? Why did you take her? Or rather why did I take her… uhhhhh…"

"As I said before, it was the only way I could get your attention. It was your pain and anger that caused her to disappear. Now we are one. There is no reason for her to be gone."

Day 3,285 (9 years later)

"Time to get up, sleepy head."

Morgan heard the sound of metal rungs being dragged across curtain rods. She felt the sun expand in the room. She turned over and saw an unfamiliar woman next to the bed.

"You were really out."

"I… I'm sorry, who are you?"

"Oh, you must have been away again. You're always a little confused when you've been traveling."

Morgan surveyed the white room. The table next to her held a phone that looked like a hotel phone. She looked at the woman standing next to the bed.

"Who are you?"

"That must have been a doozy."

"What are you talking about?"

The woman sat on the bed and placed her hand on Morgan's leg. "Sometimes when you sleep, you go out to different places, realms, other lives. You have learned to transcend time and space, but when you sleep, especially if you're tired, sometimes you don't have control over it. I think you get a little lost and you wake up confused."

Morgan struggled to sit up and took a deep breath. "Well this time I'm really confused because I still don't know who you are."

"That's ok. I'm Lena. I have been your assistant for about 5 years now. I travel with you and help make sure everything runs smoothly."

"Maybe I should ask who I am?"

Lena laughed, "Oh boy. You're Lila Das. Not to scare you, but there are a few thousand people who are looking forward to seeing you in a few hours."

"And… uh… what are they expecting me to do?"

"Heal them."

"Heal them?"

"Yes. You are a renowned healer, people come to you in droves because of what you offer."

"Uhhhhhh, ok. I sure hope I figure that out." Morgan paused and caressed the sheet in front of her wondering if it was real. "Where are we? Are we in a hotel somewhere?"

"Paris. Yes, the Palais Royale."

"Do you know Daisy?"

"Your daughter? Yes, of course, she's touring herself. We'll see her in London in two days."

"She's alive?"

"Of course. Is that where you were? You were back in your life when Daisy died?"

"I guess… I was writing or rewriting my story to try and change what happened, so that she didn't die."

"That's the story in your first book."

"How many have I written now?"

"Five."

"What about Max? Is he ok? Where is he?"

"Max is a different story..."

Day 88

The sun tickled her eyes through the window. No one had thought to draw the curtains in the darkness. Ben snored next to her. Morgan got out of bed and raced up the stairs.

Daisy's door was closed. Morgan did not hesitate to open it. There, in the bed, Daisy was splayed out in her usual fashion, taking up so much more of the bed than seemed possible for her small body. Morgan dropped to her knees, *"Thanks Ariadne, thanks my musey friends... and Luke."* The muses had followed Morgan up the stairs to Daisy's room. They bowed and backed out the door. Morgan felt Ariadne's heart hug in her chest.

Daisy opened her eyes, "Mama... are you ok?"

Morgan smiled at her little girl with tears in her eyes, "Yes, baby girl, I'm so fine. I'm great. I love you so much."

"I love you too Mama." Daisy snuggled up to Morgan. *"Now I have to go check on Max."* thought Morgan.

Epilogue

It was a hot day at the beach. A little boy built an elaborate network of sand castles. He was alone. He appeared to be four or five with shaggy blonde hair and intense blue eyes. She saw no sign of parents, siblings or friends, only the little boy digging moats and canals between castles of various sizes and shapes. Morgan watched him for a few moments without speaking. He ignored her.

"You're really good at building castles." Morgan observed. The boy showed no sign of having heard her or being aware of her at all.

Something in Morgan told her to stay, so she sat down and continued to watch the boy as his creation came to life. After a while he put his shovel down and started to walk away. He turned and looked Morgan in the eye. *"Are you coming?"* He asked in mind-speak.

"Yes," she replied.

They made their way through the crowds at the beach. The boy led and Morgan followed. Morgan noticed a rocky outcropping in the distance. They headed in that direction.

As they approached the towering rocks it grew colder as if the outcropping had its own microclimate. Unfazed, the boy in purple swimming trunks proceeded to climb. Morgan saw a cave opening above them. She followed him up the rocks.

Inside the cave was a dark void. No light penetrated past the first few feet. The boy took Morgan's hand and led her further into the cavern. After a bit they came to an open space. And though there was no source of light she could now 'see' in the darkness. There was a pool in front of them and a bench against the wall of the cave.

"This is where I come to contemplate evil. I come to sit with it, to make friends with it. It's my job."

Morgan's heart shifted into deep sadness. The weight in her chest mirrored the weight on the boy's small shoulders. She sat down and moved to pull him into her lap.

"I'm evil too," he said.

"I'm not afraid," said Morgan. *"I know that there is just as much light as darkness within you. You need your shadow in order to build your castles. The light makes them shine."*

"I need you to help me. I'm lost in the darkness."

"You led me here. You're not lost."

The boy now seated in her lap turned himself bright red to prove how evil he was. *"I am going to eat you now!"*

Morgan watched herself smile and offered him her breast to suckle. He smiled back revealing fangs. Morgan held her breast for him. He bit it and took blood and milk into his mouth. Then he ate her breast as she sat holding him. When done with her breast, he consumed her chest, but instead of bleeding, bits of light escaped the holes in Morgan's body. With each bite he exposed more of her light body. The parts where her flesh was removed sparkled in the darkness. The glittering light caused the boy to pause in his meal. He sat back and gazed up into Morgan's eyes.

"Are you full yet or do you need some more?" asked Morgan.

"There is an evil thing here with us. What do we do with it?"

"Transform it. Make it into something you can touch. Maybe a wolf with hair the color of yours."

"Okay. But green eyes, not blue."

"I like the idea of green eyes."

He jumped off Morgan's lap and went into the darkness. He came back with a wolf whose hair was the color of wheat just like the boy's, but he had green eyes.

"Try petting him."

The boy ran his fingers through the wolf's thick fur.

"Now hug him."

The boy wrapped his arms around the wolf's neck and nuzzled his face into him.

"Ask him to help you, ask him to be your protector."

Morgan watched as the boy whispered in the wolf's ear. The wolf glanced at Morgan as the boy spoke and she knew he would take care of the child. The wolf followed as they left the cave and made their way down the rocks and back to the boy's city of castles on the beach. Morgan kissed the boy on the top of the head and left them. The wolf stood watch panting in the sun.

Morgan paused and turned around to see the boy staring at her. *"You know you were a wolf once before and when you consumed me, I was transformed. So we have helped each other. Thank you."*

Morgan sat on the airplane with her computer open. It was two hours until she landed in LA. Then what? She knew Jeff's name and the name of his company. She googled the company and found an address. She could find no personal address for Jeff Christman. It was as if he did not exist. She knew what his apartment looked like from her dreams, or at least she thought she did. But how would she find it in the sprawling metropolis of LA? What was she thinking? What would she say to him if she found him?

"You will be given the knowledge you need at the time you need it. Don't worry about that now. You have made the move to find him and pursue your destiny. We will help you. You will not be alone."

"You're not Ariadne."

"No, I am a new guide for this next part of your journey. As you change, so do your guides."

"Is Ariadne gone?" Morgan checked in for the warmth in her chest which signaled Ariadne's presence.

"Not gone. She has taken a step back because this is my job."

"So I could still call on her?"

"She will always be with you even if you are unaware of her presence. She is helping you in different ways now."

"I know you guys don't go in for names so much, but what can I call you?"

"Dharin."

"Ok. Dharin. What do I do now?"

"You write down the things you need to note in your journal. Then you rest."

Three pairs of eyes peered at her over the empty seat in front. *"Did someone say write? We. Are. Here!"* They jumped up and down banging what would be their heads on the ceiling. *"We love you!!!"*

Morgan turned her attention back to the computer.

Several hours later Morgan stood in the cramped plane as everyone crowded into the aisle to get out.

"Ok Dharin, now what?"

"Now you go get a taxi."

"To where?"

"Start with Jeff's company address."

"Ok." Morgan sighed and pulled her bag forward in the aisle.

She followed all the signs to ground transportation and stepped into the hot hazy sunlight of a Los Angeles afternoon. A line of taxis snaked back from a stand where a group of people lined up. She stood at the back.

As she reached the front of the line a man handed her a piece of paper with tips for not getting cheated by the drivers. *"Nice,"* thought Morgan.

A small blue and white car pulled up and a dark haired man wearing a crisp white shirt and sharply creased, perfectly pressed khaki trousers hopped out to take her bag and put it in the trunk. He turned a bright smile to Morgan. "Where are you headed?"

"Century City." As he opened the door for Morgan to get in, she noticed his shoes. They were black woven leather, very soft, very fine. As he closed the door she noted the black skin belt he wore. The cab had been painted such a funny color she had not seen that it was a Mercedes. *"That's unusual for a cab in LA."*

She caught the driver's eye in the rearview mirror. "I'm Mario."

"Morgan." She said as he pulled into the lane to exit the airport.

"That's not what I would call you."

Morgan could see her face reflected in the rearview mirror next to the top of his head. "I'm sorry. What did you say?"

"I said that's not what I would call you."

"Ok. What would you call me?"

Mario turned his head to glance at Morgan as he drove. "I would call you Lila Das."

"How do you know that name? I've never told anyone that."

"I know."

"So what else do you know?"

"I know you have come looking for him, your counterpart. The Divine Male alchemist."

"How do you know all this?"

"Because it's my job. I'm a Facilitator."

"I don't know what you mean."

"There are many of us. Unlike you I have been aware for quite some time. But I, like you, have to wait until things shift in order to act. I have been waiting to do my job, to facilitate the Things That Must Be. I help them happen."

Morgan sat in silence. She looked out the window. They were on a twelve lane highway creeping along at five miles an hour.

Mario glanced out at the traffic. "It will give us plenty of time to talk privately. I know you have questions. I'm at your service."

"I understand that my name is also my job. I know that the Lila is the 'play of the Universe' and something to do with the sexual tension between Krishna and Radha, the Hindu deities. But I don't understand what that means for me."

"The Lila is the tension of creation. It is the tension between the divine male and female energies, the shadow and the light, that brings all creation and all transformation. 'Das' means servant or devotee. Your job is to balance the forces of creation and destruction."

Morgan laughed, "Well, that sounds easy. What the hell does that mean?"

"Creation can only happen when the energies are properly balanced so that the tension is right. Those energies have been out of balance for several millennia. It's your job to fix that."

"And how the hell do I do that?"

"One step at a time."

"What's the first step?"

"You already completed the first step. You balanced yourself. The second is finding him."

"But he ran away. And I think he knows what he's supposed to be doing. He has been aware his whole life. I'm just now figuring all this out. Why do I have to do this?"

The traffic had come to a standstill. Mario turned around to look at Morgan. "He's been aware long enough to have paid a great price in this lifetime. He is well aware of the price he has paid in many lifetimes. He does not want to do this job, as he understands the danger. There are those who will fight to keep things the way they are. They do not want you to succeed. He is very attached to his comfortable life; he is protective of his kids, even his ex-wife. He knows that once you are aware there is no turning back if he joins forces with you, but for now he's hiding. He's a very reluctant alchemist. It's your job to draw him out."

"Maybe I should be scared. I love my kids too. That's part of the reason I'm here."

"Oh no, not you, Lila Das. You're fierce. You know in your heart it's all a game. That's your name. It's who you truly are. You know deep down that you are protected and that if you follow your guidance all will be as it should. Keep following your heart. Neither your soul nor the souls of your children or anyone you care for can be killed. Your body may pass, but it is nothing. He has been so long in hiding, hiding even from himself, that he has forgotten much of what he knew."

"I'm still scared. I still don't think I have any idea what I'm doing."

"And that's why you have Dharin and others guiding you. And now you have me. You will have all the help you need. You have to have faith when things get well... busy, that it will all be alright."

They pulled up to an empty lot surrounded by a fence sporting signs announcing a new condominium complex.

"Is this the address of his office?"

"Yes, see." He showed her the address in his phone.

"How do I know this isn't some sort of a trick?"

Mario laughed. "Well, I knew your name, your real name, so maybe that's worth some amount of trust."

"Ok. What now?"

"Do you want to see where he used to live?"

"Used to live? How do you know? Oh, nevermind. Yes."

Forty-five minutes later they pulled up to a towering black building. Morgan could see the green park on the other side. The one she had seen from the balcony in her yoga class visions. She shook her head.

"Look familiar?"

It was Morgan's turn to laugh. "Yes. It does. I don't know which floor it was, but it seemed pretty high up. I'd recognize the décor too."

"Not anymore. He cleaned it out. When he broke with you, he shut it all down."

"Where is he now?"

"He has the power to completely cloak and he has gone underground. He knows about us. He has always avoided us, but now he's in hiding. That's why we need you."

"Us?"

'The Awakened."

"He mentioned that when I first met him. I thought you sounded like vampires or something. Then Morgan thought, "*Maybe I shouldn't trust you... he didn't.*"

"You thought you came to LA to find him, but the Universe wanted you to find me. You needed to set that intention, finding him. You did. Now you need to finish that book. That's how you are going to find him."

"But that will betray him. I will only be betraying him again. It's what he most fears. It's why he's hiding from me now."

"It will not be a betrayal. You'll see. Have faith you will find a way to do this so that he will respond, but no one will know."

"You're saying I am going to write a book, and publish it and then he will not feel betrayed and he will respond and do what he needs to do with me. Are you nuts? Why don't I just take out an ad in the New York Times? Jeff Christman, Male Alchemist of the Christ Energy, where the fuck are you? This is fucking nuts."

"Ahhh, there's that sailor's mouth I heard about." Mario chuckled and shook his head as he leaned against the car. "It will be the right way. It won't take long to write the book. Everything will be as it should. You'll see. Have faith Lila Das. Remember it's all a game. We don't always understand why, we just have to play our parts and let the Universe take care of the rest. Come on let's get you back to the airport. You have other things to do."

CPSIA information can be obtained
at www.ICGtesting.com
Printed in the USA
BVHW092127291120
594452BV00012B/276